Appalachian Writers

PRENTICE HALL
Upper Saddle River, New Jersey
Needham, Massachusetts
Glenview, Illinois

ISBN 0-13-009974-0

3 4 5 6 7 8 9 10 03 02 01

PRENTICE HALL

Acknowledgments

Grateful acknowledgment is made to the following for copyrighted material:

J.J. Augustin Inc.
"Barbara Allen" from *Folk Songs from the Southern Highlands,* compiled by Mellinger Edward Henry. J.J. Augustin, publisher, 1938. Reprinted by permission of the publisher.

Berea College Press
"Heritage" from *The Wolfpen Poems* by James Still. Copyright 1983. Reprinted by permission of Berea College Press.

Wendell Berry c/o The Spieler Agency
"The Memory of Old Jack" from *The Memory of Old Jack* by Wendell Berry. Copyright © 1974 by Wendell Berry. "Her First Calf" by Wendell Berry from *Collected Poems,* North Point Press. Copyright © 1984 by Wendell Berry. Reprinted with permission of the author.

Educational Broadcasting Corporation, Bill Moyers and William Morris Agency for the Estate of Robert Penn Warren
From "A Conversation with Robert Penn Warren" by Bill Moyers, broadcast on WNET Thirteen, 1976. Copyright © 1976 by Educational Broadcasting Corporation. Reprinted courtesy of Thirteen/WNET New York.

Farrar, Straus & Giroux, Inc.
"The Elect" from *The Collected Stories* by Peter Taylor. Copyright © 1968 by Peter Taylor. Reprinted by permission of Farrar, Straus & Giroux, Inc.

Gnomon Press
From *Newfound* by Jim Wayne Miller. Copyright © 1989, 1996 by Jim Wayne Miller. Published by Gnomon Press, 1996. Reprinted by permission of Gnomon Press.

Gail Godwin
"Uncle Orphy" by Gail Godwin from *Bloodroot: Reflections on Place by Appalachian Women Writers,* edited by Joyce Dyer. Reprinted by permission of the author.

(Acknowledgments continue on p. 186.)

Contents

Introduction

This anthology represents a steady progression from the values and cultural beliefs of the old pre-Civil War South, to the new South—a society which accepts growth, accepts industry, and the qualities of modern life, while holding on to all that is established as good in the past. These themes are presented through the words of writers whose personal experience and acute awareness of civilization has given meaning to the personalities and lives of southern Appalachian people.

Genuinely southern Appalachian writers are usually recognizable. They almost necessarily grew up in the South. Because they feel a strong bond with their heritage, they are for the most part reluctant to discard the ideals of past generations. Even if they no longer completely accepts these beliefs themselves, they are nevertheless ready to defend them as worthy when seen in a historical perspective. Although they may live in later years outside of the South, their writing continues to draw upon these early experiences. Most of the writers in the present volume fit such a description, at least approximately.

On April 9, 1865, at Appomattox Courthouse, General Robert E. Lee accepted the surrender terms that were offered by Union General Ulysses S. Grant, bringing an end to the Civil War. To many Southern people the loss of the Civil War was the defining moment of their lives. Their home—the South, depleted of economic and natural resources—was in ruins. Richmond, Atlanta, and other major cities had been burned to the ground. Universities, such as William and Mary and the University of North Carolina, suffered a similar fate. Railways and factories also were demolished, and fields lay barren.

As the South recovered over the next few decades, one of greatest changes in southern life was the shift from a predominantly agricultural economy to an industrial one. Southern authors have dealt seriously with this change. Some have rejoiced in the modern industrialization, arguing that the South should embrace the twentieth century. Others have disapproved of the transition on the basis that not everything their ancestors believed in was wholly bad. Still others have challenged us to face contemporary issues and essentially ignore past traditions. These several attitudes among the authors express the convictions of a new southern society. It might be said that the predominant link connecting the majority of the selections in the present volume is a society in transition and the quest for one's place in the world.

It is against this background that we read the opening selection of the anthology, Donald Davidson's "Lee in the Mountains," a poem of hope in light of an uncertain future. Here you will see Robert E. Lee, no longer a war general but a man who ironically walks "in a dark civilian suit." He reflects upon the war and the unalterable change that has taken place in the South. Although Lee must stand "without arms or men," he is compensated with knowledge: to accept what cannot be changed and continue the business of living, with the hope that one day a new life will "flower among the hills to which we cleave."

Just as Donald Davidson's lament over the loss of the Civil War is written in a dramatic voice, Thomas Wolfe's lyrically written short story "The Four Lost Men" is also grimly serious. Here, false claims of heroism, glamour, and glory are exposed by the memory of four soldiers whose lives are permanently altered by the war that "gives life to men as well as death." We see, in Wolfe's story, characters who are displaced from their normal lives and struggle to adapt to their new surroundings. In a progressing society, there is an unavoidable clash between new values and the traditions that have sustained it for countless generations. This conflict arises in Ellen Glasgow's "Jordan's End," where the protagonist defies the laws of society when she chooses to obey her southern heritage and remain loyal to her husband.

Whereas identity in "Jordan's End" is expressed in the strength to withstand modern values, the opposite holds true for William Wells Brown, an ex-slave who gains his individuality by rejecting the laws of an old order. Paul Green's play "In Abraham's Bosom," chronicles an African American's struggle for self-realization and enlightenment in a growing society, where education and the position one maintains in the world are explicitly linked. The value of widening one's horizons is further expressed in Elizabeth Madox Roberts's "On the Mountainside," a story that depicts a young man who, after coming into contact with a man of learning, is prompted to begin a journey in quest of knowledge and the freedom which he imagines can be found in the outside world.

The value of education is a strong focus of the children born after the Civil War, but the majority of their forbears—as seen in Jesse Stuart's tribute to his father "The Earth Poet"—learning had a broader application, coming from a love and appreciation of the land. The next four poems, Stuart's "Our Heritage," James Still's "Heritage," Wendell Berry's "Her First Calf," and Robert Penn Warren's "Caribou," further enforce this idea while linking it to the mystery of nature. This last sentiment is memorably stated in Warren's poem as the speaker observes of the caribou—"I have lost the spot. I find only blankness / But / They must have been going somewhere."

This "somewhere," as the speaker says, we can never know, yet authors have made the attempt to look back and discover the influences that have shaped their lives. Wendell Berry's "The Memory of Old Jack," Gail Godwin's "Uncle Orphy," and "Adios, Miss Em," by Janice Holt Giles all examine close relationships between people. In "Adios, Miss Em," three young boys spend the summer in the orchard of an elderly woman; she is irritated by the disruption the boys present to her calm, silent life. But eventually, she begins to take part in their imaginative games, and as the days of summer pass, their bond of friendship grows. When September arrives and the family makes plans to move on, she is startled by her attachment to them: "Miss Em waved, too, as long as she could see them, and just as the car turned onto the highway called, although they could not hear, 'Goodbye! Goodbye!'"

Love and death are represented through three genres—fiction, folk songs, and poetry. The first selection, "Wild Plums" by Jesse Stuart is a short story concerning the promise of youth and of man's joy in the annual renewal of life in the spring. A different attitude is given in the excerpt from the novel *Newfound* by Jim Wayne Miller, where the bitter pangs of a young man's unreciprocated love are skillfully expressed through the symbolic chinquapin pepper. Striking a distinctly similar note are the folk songs "Barbara Allen" and "Why Can't I take Love Easy?" and the two poems of Joseph S. Cotter, Jr., "An April Day" and "Memories." The folk songs represent, as does Miller's *Newfound,* a tragic aspect of a human love experience, but Cotter's poems, like Stuart's "Wild Plums," sees love as a life-giving principle.

The idea of death is expressed in A. R. Ammons's "Hardweed Path Going," as the impending death of a well-beloved hog troubles the mind of a young boy. Joe Survant's "The Fish" describes the catching and scaling of a great fish, and the speaker of Jim Wayne Miller's "Squirrel Stand" reflects upon his mortality: "My days were growing full, sliding, dropping / like waterbeads along the barbed-wire fence."

All of the authors in this present volume, to a greater or lesser degree, explore modern themes and propose questions concerning the fate of the individual. The short piece by Thomas Wolfe illustrates the uncertainty of the modern man who, when stripped of the inaccuracies that delude his perspective, is left with the discomforting view of reality. "And he knew that all the magic of the bright lost way . . . could never be got again," is the painful realization of "The Far and the Near."

This burden of reality and the fate of the individual is dramatized throughout the remaining selections—from "A Conversation with Robert Penn Warren," a dialogue discussing man's need of literature and history to avoid becoming a slave to technology, to Doris Betts's "All that Glisters Isn't Gold," which explores a young girl's dilemma between religion and science. Warren's "The Patented Gate and the Mean Hamburger" examines a relationship highlighting technology (a man who buys a patented gate) and business (his wife who becomes the owner of a burger house). In Peter Taylor's "The Elect," the ambitions of a governor-elect threaten his wife's humanity.

The next two excerpts confront the interrelationship between gender, race, and society. George Ella Lyon's "Voiceplace" is an essay that expresses the importance of maintaining one's differences. In "Parable of the Talents" by Henry Louis Gates Jr., the author reveals one African American's fear of being able to succeed in an ivy league college.

In Bobbie Ann Mason's *In Country* the author depicts a teenaged Kentucky girl who becomes determined to find out her late father's experiences in the Vietnam War. The novel excerpt by Mason and Robert Penn Warren's "If Snakes were Blue," both acknowledge the difficulty and unfairness of life, yet maintain the conviction that, in the distance, one can always see the hope and promise yet to come.

In all of these works, the strong bond between the writers and their heritage is evident. The themes of one selection frequently lead into and further examine the ones following, so that they read not so much as separate pieces, but rather one continuous volume, wherein authors are engaged in rediscovering a uniquely southern Appalachian voice—one that acknowledges the past and its influence on the present, and one that strives to understand the individual's place in a complicated society.

Appalachian Writers

Lee in the Mountains

Donald Davidson

After the surrender of Appomattox, Robert E. Lee was offered and accepted the presidency of Washington College in Lexington, Virginia. He held the position until his death in 1870. The mountains mentioned in the title of the poem refer both to mountains of North Carolina, where Lee had hoped to escape in the closing days of the Civil War, and the mountains near the university, where he spent the remaining days of his life.

Walking into the shadows, walking alone
Where the sun falls through the ruined boughs of locusts
Up to the president's office. . . .
                                        Hearing the voices
Whisper, *Hush, it is General Lee!* And strangely
Hearing my own voice say, *Good morning, boys.*
(Don't get up. You are early. It is long
Before the bell. You will have long to wait
On these cold steps. . . .)
                                The young have time to wait.
But soldiers' faces under their tossing flags
Lift no more by any road or field,
And I am spent with old wars and new sorrow.
Walking the rocky path, where steps decay
And the paint cracks and grass eats on the stone.
It is not General Lee, young men. . . .
It is Robert Lee in a dark civilian suit who walks,
An outlaw fumbling for the latch, a voice
Commanding in a dream where no flag flies.

My father's house is taken and his hearth
Left to the candle-drippings where the ashes
Whirl at a chimney-breath on the cold stone.
I can hardly remember my father's look, I cannot
Answer his voice as he calls farewell in the misty
Mounting where riders gather at gates.
He was old then—I was a child—his hand
Held out for mine, some daybreak snatched away,

And he rode out, a broken man. Now let
His lone grave keep, surer than cypress roots,
The vow I made beside him. God too late
Unseals to certain eyes the drift
Of time and the hopes of men and a sacred cause.
The fortune of the Lees goes with the land
Whose sons will keep it still. My mother
Told me much. She sat among the candles,
Fingering the *Memoirs*, now so long unread.[1]
And as my pen moves on across the page
Her voice comes back, a murmuring distillation
Of old Virginia times now faint and gone,
The hurt of all that was and cannot be.

Why did my father write? I know he saw
History clutched as a wraith out of blowing mist
Where tongues are loud, and a glut of little souls
Laps at the too much blood and the burning house.
He would have his say, but I shall not have mine.
What I do is only a son's devoir
To a lost father. Let him only speak.
The rest must pass to men who never knew
(But on a written page) the strike of armies,
And never heard the long Confederate cry
Charge through the muzzling smoke or saw the bright
Eyes of the beardless boys go up to death.
It is Robert Lee who writes with his father's hand—
The rest must go unsaid and the lips be locked.

If all were told, as it cannot be told—
If all the dread opinion of the heart
Now could speak, now in the shame and torment
Lashing the bound and trampled States—

If a word were said, as it cannot be said—
I see clear waters run in Virginia's Valley
And in the house the weeping of young women
Rises no more. The waves of grain begin.
The Shenandoah is golden with new grain.

1. *Memoirs,* now so long unread: During Lee's time as president at Washington College, he edited and republished the memoirs written by his father, Henry Lee, a hero of the Revolutionary War. Lee's edition, *Memoirs of the War in the Southern Department of the United States,* was published in 1869.

The Blue Ridge, crowned with a haze of light,
Thunders no more. The horse is at plough. The rifle
Returns to the chimney crotch and the hunter's hand.
And nothing else than this? Was it for this
That on an April day we stacked our arms
Obedient to a soldier's trust? To lie
Ground by heels of little men,
Forever maimed, defeated, lost, impugned?
And was I then betrayed? Did I betray?

If it were said, as still it might be said—
If it were said, and a word should run like fire,
Like living fire into the roots of grass,
The sunken flag would kindle on wild hills,
The brooding hearts would waken, and the dream
Stir like a crippled phantom under the pines,
And this torn earth would quicken into shouting
Beneath the feet of ragged bands—
The pen
Turns to the waiting page, the sword
Bows to the rust that cankers and the silence.

Among these boys whose eyes lift up to mine
Within gray walls where droning wasps repeat
A hollow reveille, I still must face,
Day after day, the courier with his summons
Once more to surrender, now to surrender all.
Without arms or men I stand, but with knowledge only
I face what long I saw, before others knew,
When Pickett's men streamed back, and I heard the tangled
Cry of the Wilderness wounded, bloody with doom.

The mountains, once I said, in the little room
At Richmond, by the huddled fire, but still
The President shook his head. The mountains wait,
I said, in the long beat and rattle of siege
At cratered Petersburg. Too late
We sought the mountains and those people came.
And Lee is in mountains now, beyond Appomattox,
Listening long for voices that never will speak
Again; hearing the hoofbeats come and go and fade
Without a stop, without a brown hand lifting
The tent-flap, or a bugle call at dawn,

Or ever on the long white road the flag
Of Jackson's quick brigades. I am alone,
Trapped, consenting, taken at last in mountains.

It is not the bugle now, or the long roll beating.
The simple stroke of a chapel bell forbids
The hurtling dream, recalls the lonely mind.
Young men, the God of your fathers is a just
And merciful God Who in this blood once shed
On your green altars measures out all days,
And measures out the grace
Whereby alone we live;
And in His might He waits,
Brooding within the certitude of time,
To bring this lost forsaken valor
And the fierce faith undying
And the love quenchless
To flower among the hills to which we cleave,
To fruit upon the mountains whither we flee,
Never forsaking, never denying
His children and His children's children forever
Unto all generations of the faithful heart.

from

The Four Lost Men

Thomas Wolfe

SUDDENLY, at the green heart of June, I heard my father's voice again. That year I was sixteen; the week before I had come home from my first year at college, and the huge thrill and menace of war, which we had entered just two months before, had filled our hearts. And war gives life to men as well as death. It fills the hearts of young men with wild song and jubilation. It wells up in their throats in great-starred night the savage goat-cry of their pain and joy. And it fills them with a wild and wordless prophecy not of death, but life, for it speaks to them of new lands, triumph, and discovery, of heroic deeds, the fame and fellowship of heroes, and the love of glorious unknown women—of shining triumph and a grand success in a heroic world, and of a life more fortunate and happy than they have ever known.

So it was with us all that year. Over the immense and waiting earth, the single pulse and promise of the war impended. One felt it in the little towns at dawn, with all their quiet, casual, utterly familiar acts of life beginning. One felt it in the route-boy deftly flinging the folded block of paper on a porch, a man in shirt-sleeves coming out upon the porch and bending for the paper, the slow-clopping hoofs of the milk horse in a quiet street, the bottle-clinking wagon, and the sudden pause, the rapid footsteps of the milkman and the clinking bottles, then clopping hoof and wheel, and morning, stillness, the purity of light, and the dew-sweet bird-song rising in the street again.

In all these ancient, ever-new, unchanging, always magic acts of life and light and morning one felt the huge impending presence of the war. And one felt it in the brooding hush of noon, in the warm, dusty stir and flutter of the feathery clucking of the sun-warm hens at noon. One felt it in the ring of the ice-tongs in the street, the cool whine of the ice-saws droning through the smoking block. One felt it poignantly somehow, in the solid lonely liquid leather shuffle of men in shirt-sleeves coming home to lunch in one direction in the brooding hush and time-enchanted spell of noon, and in the screens that slammed and sudden silence. And one felt it in the humid warmth and hungry fragrance of the cooking turnip greens, in leaf and blade and flower, in smell of tar, and the sudden haunting green-gold summer absence of the street-car after it had gone.

In all these ancient, most familiar things and acts and colors of our lives, one felt, with numbing ecstasy, the impending presence of the war. The war had got in everything: it was in things that moved, and in things that were still, in the animate red silence of an old brick wall as well as in the thronging life and traffic of the streets. It was in the faces of the people passing and in the thousand familiar moments of man's daily life and business.

And lonely, wild, and haunting, calling us on forever with the winding of its far lost horn, it had got into the time-enchanted loneliness of the magic hills around us, in all the sudden, wild, and lonely lights that came and passed and vanished on the massed green of the wilderness.

The war was in far cries and broken sounds and cow bells tinkling in the gusty wind, and in the far, wild, wailing joy and sorrow of a departing train, as it rushed eastward, seaward, war-ward through a valley of the South in the green spell and golden magic of full June. The war was in the ancient red-gold light of fading day that fell without violence or heat upon the streets of life, the houses where men lived, the brief flame and fire of sheeted window panes.

And it was in field and gulch and hollow, in the sweet green mountain valleys, fading into dusk, and in the hill-flanks reddened with the ancient light and slanting fast into steep cool shade and lilac silence. It was in the whole earth breathing the last heat and weariness of day out in the huge hush and joy and sorrow of oncoming night.

Finally, the war had gotten into all sounds and secrecies, the sorrow, longing, and delight, the mystery, hunger, and wild joy that came from the deep-breasted heart of fragrant, all-engulfing night. It was in the sweet and secret rustling of the leaves in summer streets, in footsteps coming quiet, slow, and lonely along the darkness of a leafy street, in screen doors slammed, and silence, the distant barking of a dog, far voices, laughter, faint pulsing music at a dance, and in all the casual voices of the night, far, strangely near, most intimate and familiar, remote as time, as haunting as the briefness of our days.

And suddenly, as I sat there under the proud and secret mystery of huge-starred, velvet-breasted night, hearing my father's great voice sounding from the porch again, the war, with a wild and intolerable loneliness of ecstasy and desire, came to me in the sudden throbbing of a racing motor, far-away silence, an image of the cool sweet darkness of the mountainside, the white flesh and yielding tenderness of women. And even as I thought of this, I heard the low, rich, sensual welling of a woman's voice, voluptuous, low, and tender, from the darkness of a summer porch across the street.

What had the war changed? What had it done to us? What miracle of transformation had it wrought upon our lives? It had changed nothing; it had heightened, intensified, and made glorious all the ancient and familiar things of life. It had added hope to hope, joy to joy, and life to life; and from that vital wizardry it had rescued all our lives from hopelessness and despair, and made us live again who thought that we were lost.

The war seemed to have collected in a single image of joy, and power, and proud compacted might all of the thousand images of joy and power and all-exulting life which we had always had, and for which we had never had a word before. Over the fields of silent and mysterious night it seemed that we could hear the nation marching, that we could hear, soft and thunderous in the night, the million-footed unison of marching men. And that single, glorious image of all-collected joy and unity and might had given new life and hope to all of us.

My father was old, he was sick with a cancer that flowered and fed forever at his entrails, eating from day to day the gaunt sinew of his life away beyond a hope or remedy, and we knew that he was dying. Yet under the magic life and hope the war had brought to us, his life seemed to have revived again out of its grief and pain, its death of joy, its sorrow of irrevocable memory.

For a moment he seemed to live again in his full prime. And instantly we were all released from the black horror of death and time that had menaced us for years. Instantly we were freed from the evil spell of sorrowful time and memory that had made his living death more horrible than his real one could ever be.

And instantly the good life, the golden and jubilant life of childhood, in whose full magic we had been sustained by the power of his life, and which had seemed so lost and irrevocable that it had a dreamlike strangeness when we thought of it, had under this sudden flare of life and joy and war returned in all its various and triumphant colors. And for a moment we believed that all would be again for us as it had been, that he never could grow old and die, but that he must live forever, and that the summertime, the orchard and bright morning, would be ours again, could never die.

I could hear him talking now about old wars and ancient troubles, hurling against the present and its leaders the full indictment of his soaring rhetoric that howled, rose, fell, swept out into the night, piercing all quarters of the darkness with the naked penetration which his voice had in the old days when he sat talking on the porch in summer darkness, and the neighborhood attended and was still.

Now as my father talked, I could hear the boarders on the porch attending in the same way, the stealthy creak of a rocker now and then, a low word spoke, a question, protest, or agreement, and then their hungry, feeding, and attentive silence as my father talked. He spoke of all the wars and troubles he had known, told how he had stood, "a bare-foot country boy," beside a dusty road twelve miles from Gettysburg and had watched the ragged rebels march past upon the road that led to death and battle and the shipwreck of their hopes.

He spoke of the faint and ominous trembling of the guns across the hot brooding silence of the countryside, and how silence, wonder, and unspoken questions filled the hearts of all the people, and how they had gone about their work on the farm as usual. He spoke of the years that had followed on the war when he was a stone-cutter's apprentice in Baltimore, and he spoke of ancient joys and labors, forgotten acts and histories, and he spoke then with familiar memory of the lost Americans—the strange, lost, time-far, dead Americans, the remote, voiceless, and bewhiskered faces of the great Americans, who were more lost to me than Egypt, more far from me than the Tartarian coasts, more haunting strange than Cipango or the lost faces of the first dynastic kings that built the Pyramids—and whom he had seen, heard, known, found familiar in the full pulse, and passion, and proud glory of his youth: the lost, time-far, voiceless faces of Buchanan, Johnson, Douglas, Blaine—the proud, vacant, time-strange and bewhiskered faces of Garfield, Arthur, Harrison, and Hayes. . . .[1]

"Ah, Lord!" he muttered, shaking his head sadly, thinly, wearily in the dark. "I've seen them all. . . . I've seen them come and go . . . Garfield, Arthur, Harrison, and Hayes . . . and all . . . all . . . all of them are dead. . . . I'm the only one that's left," he

1. Garfield, Arthur, Harrison, and Hayes.: James Abram Garfield (1831–1881), Chester Alan Arthur (1829–1886), Benjamin Harrison (1833–1901), and Rutherford B. Hayes (1822–1893) are American Presidents who, before becoming presidents, served in the Civil War.

said illogically, "and soon I'll be gone, too." And for a moment he was silent. "It's pretty strange when you come to think of it," he muttered. "By God it is!" And he was silent, and darkness, and mystery, and night were all about us.

Garfield, Arthur, Harrison, and Hayes—time of my father's time, blood of his blood, life of his life, had been living, real, and actual people in all the passion, power, and feeling of my father's youth. And for me they were the lost Americans: their gravely vacant and bewhiskered faces mixed, melted, swam together in the sea-depths of a past intangible, immeasurable, and unknowable as the buried city of Persepolis.

And they were lost.

For who was Garfield, martyred man, and who had seen him in the streets of life? Who could believe his footfalls ever sounded on a lonely pavement? Who had heard the casual and familiar tones of Chester Arthur? And where was Harrison? Where was Hayes? Which had the whiskers, which the burnsides: which was which?

Were they not lost?

Into their ears, as ours, the tumults of forgotten crowds, upon their brains the million printings of lost time, and suddenly upon their dying sight the brief, bitter pain and joy of a few death-bright, fixed, and fading memories: the twisting of a leaf upon a bough, the grinding felloe-rim[2] against the curb, the long, and distant retreating thunder of a train upon the rails.

Garfield, Hayes, and Harrison were Ohio men; but only the name of Garfield has been brightened by his blood. But at night had they not heard the howlings of demented wind, the sharp, clean, windy raining to the earth of acorns? Had all of them not walked down lonely roads at night in winter and seen a light and known it was theirs?

Had they not known the smell of old bound calf and well-worn leathers, the Yankee lawyer's smell of strong tobacco spit and court-house urinals, the smell of horses, harness, hay, and sweating country men, of jury rooms and court rooms—the strong male smell of justice at the county seat, and heard a tap along dark corridors where a drop fell in darkness with a punctual crescent monotone of time, dark time?

Had not Garfield, Hayes, and Harrison studied law in offices with a dark brown smell? Had not the horses trotted past below

2. felloe-rim: The rim of a spoked wheel.

their windows in wreaths of dust along a straggling street of shacks and buildings with false fronts? Had they not heard below them the voices of men talking, loitering up in drawling heat? Had they not heard the casual, rich-fibered, faintly howling country voices, and heard the rustling of a woman's skirt, and waiting silence, slyly lowered tones of bawdry and then huge guffaws, slapped meaty thighs, and high, fat, choking laughter? And in the dusty dozing heat, while time buzzed slowly, like a fly, had not Garfield, Arthur, Harrison, and Hayes then smelled the river, the humid, subtly fresh, half-rotten river, and thought of the women then beside the river, and felt a slow, impending passion in their entrails, a heavy rending power in their hands?

Then Garfield, Arthur, Harrison, and Hayes had gone to war, and each became a brigadier or major general. All were bearded men: they saw a spattering of bright blood upon the leaves, and they heard the soldiers talking in the dark of food and women. They held the bridge-head in bright dust at places with such names as Wilson's Mill and Spangler's Run, and their men smashed cautiously through dense undergrowth. And they heard the surgeons cursing after battle and the little rasp of saws. They had seen boys standing awkwardly holding their entrails in their hands, and pleading pitifully with fear-bright eyes: "Is it bad, General? Do you think it's bad?"

When the canister came through, it made a ragged hole. It smashed through tangled leaves and boughs; sometimes it plunked solidly into the fiber of a tree. Sometimes when it struck a man, it tore away the roof of his brain, the wall of his skull, raggedly, so that his brains seethed out upon a foot of wilderness, and the blood blackened and congealed, and he lay there in his thick clumsy uniform, with a smell of urine in the wool, in the casual, awkward, and incompleted attitude of sudden death. And when Garfield, Arthur, Harrison, and Hayes saw these things, they saw that it was not like the picture they had had as children; it was not like the works of Walter Scott and William Gilmore Simms. They saw that the hole was not clean and small and in the central front, and the field was not green nor fenced, nor mown. Over the vast and immemorable earth the quivering heated light of afternoon was shining, a field swept rudely upward to a lift of rugged wood, and field by field, gulley by gulch by fold, the earth advanced in rude, sweet, limitless convolutions.

Then Garfield, Arthur, Harrison, and Hayes had paused by the bridgehead for a moment and were still, seeing the bright blood at noon upon the trampled wheat, feeling the brooding hush of six o'clock across the fields where all the storming feet had passed at dawn, seeing the way the rough field hedge leaned out across the dusty road, the casual intrusions of the coarse field grasses and the hot, dry daisies to the edges of the road, seeing the rock-bright shallows of the creek, the sweet cool shade and lean of river trees across the water.

They paused then by the bridge-head, looking at the water. They saw the stark blank flatness of the old red mill that somehow was like sunset, coolness, sorrow, and delight, and looking at the faces of the dead boys among the wheat, the most-oh-most familiar plain, the death-strange faces of the dead Americans, they stood there for a moment, thinking, feeling, thinking, with strong wordless wonder in their hearts:

"As we leaned on the sills of evening, as we stood in the frames of the marvelous doors, as we were received into silence, the flanks of the slope and the slanted light, as we saw the strange hushed shapes upon the land, the muted distances, knowing all things then—what could we say except that our comrades were spread quietly around us and that noon was far?

"What can we say now of the lonely land—what can we say now of the deathless shapes and substances—what can we say who have lived here with our lives, bone, blood, and brain, and all our tongueless languages, hearing on many a casual road the plain familiar voices of Americans, and tomorrow will be buried in the earth, knowing the fields will steep to silence after us, the slant light deepen on the slopes, and peace and evening will come back again, at one now with the million shapes and single substance of our land, at one with evening, peace, the huge stride of the undulant oncoming night, at one, also, with morning?

"Silence receive us and the field of peace, hush of the measureless land, the unabated distances, shape of the one and single substance and the million forms, replenish us, restore us, and unite us with your vast images of quietness and joy. Stride of the undulant night, come swiftly now, engulf us, silence, in your great-starred secrecy; speak to our hearts of stillness, for we have, save this, no speech.

"There is the bridge we crossed, the mill we slept in, and the creek. There is a field of wheat, a hedge, a dusty road, an apple orchard, and the sweet wild tangle of a wood upon that hill. And there is six o'clock across the fields again, now and always as it was and will be to the world's end forever. And some of us have died this morning coming through the field—and that was time—time—time. We shall not come again, we never shall come back again as we did once at morning—so, brothers, let us look again before we go. . . . There is the mill, and there the hedge, and there the shallows of the rock-bright waters of the creek, and there the sweet and most familiar coolness of the trees—and surely we have been this way before!" they cried.

"Oh, surely, brothers, we have sat upon the bridge, before the mill, and sung together by the rock-bright waters of the creek at evening, and come across the wheat field in the morning and heard the dew-sweet bird-song rising from the hedge before! You plain, oh-most-familiar and most homely earth, proud earth of this huge land unutterable, proud nobly swelling earth, in all your delicacy, wildness, savagery, and terror—grand earth in all your loneliness, beauty and wild joy, terrific earth in all your limitless fecundities, swelling with infinite fold and convolution into the reaches of the west forever—American earth!—bridge, hedge, and creek and dusty road—you plain tremendous poetry of Wilson's Mill where boys died in the wheat this morning—you unutterable far-near, strange-familiar, homely earth of magic, for which a word would do if we could find it, for which a word would do if we could call it by its name, for which a word would do which never can be spoken, that can never be forgotten, and that will never be revealed—oh, proud, familiar, nobly swelling earth, it seems we must have known you before! It seems that we must have known you forever, but all we know for certain is that we came along this road one time at morning, and now our blood is painted on the wheat, and you are ours now, we are yours forever—and there is something here we never shall remember—there is something here we never shall forget!"

Jordan's End

Ellen Glasgow

AT last the woods ended abruptly on the edge of an abandoned field which was thickly sown with scrub pine and broomsedge. The glow in the sky had faded now to a thin yellow-green, and a melancholy twilight pervaded the landscape. In this twilight I looked over the few sheep huddled together on the ragged lawn, and saw the old brick house crumbling beneath its rank growth of ivy. As I drew nearer I had the feeling that the surrounding desolation brooded there like some sinister influence.

Forlorn as it appeared at this first approach, I surmised that Jordan's End must have possessed once charm as well as distinction. The proportions of the Georgian front were impressive, and there was beauty of design in the quaint doorway, and in the steps of rounded stone which were brocaded now with a pattern of emerald moss. But the whole place was badly in need of repair. Looking up, as I stopped, I saw that the eaves were falling away, that crumbled shutters were sagging from loosened hinges, that odd scraps of hemp sacking or oil cloth were stuffed into windows where panes were missing. When I stepped on the floor of the porch, I felt the rotting boards give way under my feet.

After thundering vainly on the door, I descended the steps, and followed the beaten path that led round the west wing of the house. When I had passed an old boxwood tree at the corner, I saw a woman and a boy of nine years or so come out of a shed, which I took to be the smokehouse, and begin to gather chips from the woodpile. The woman carried a basket made of splits on her arm, and while she stooped to fill this, she talked to the child in a soft musical voice. Then, at a sound that I made, she put the basket aside, and rising to her feet, faced me in the pallid light from the sky. Her head was thrown back, and over her dress of some dark calico, a tattered gray shawl clung to her figure. That was thirty years ago; I am not young any longer; I have been in many countries since then, and looked on many women; but her face, with that wan light on it, is the last one I shall forget in my life. Beauty! Why, that woman will be beautiful when she is a skeleton, was the thought that flashed into my mind.

She was very tall, and so thin that her flesh seemed faintly luminous, as if an inward light pierced the transparent substance. It was the beauty, not of earth, but of triumphant spirit. Perfection, I suppose, is the rarest thing we achieve in this world of incessant compromise with inferior forms; yet the woman who stood there in that ruined place appeared to me to have stepped straight out of legend or allegory. The contour of her face was Italian in its pure oval; her hair swept in wings of dusk above her clear forehead; and, from the faintly shadowed hollows beneath her brows, the eyes that looked at me were purple-black, like dark pansies.

"I had given you up," she began in a low voice, as if she were afraid of being overheard. "You are the doctor?"

"Yes, I am the doctor. I took the wrong road and lost my way. Are you Mrs. Jordan?"

She bowed her head. "Mrs. Alan Jordan. There are three Mrs. Jordans besides myself. My husband's grandmother and the wives of his two uncles."

"And it is your husband who is ill?"

"My husband, yes. I wrote a few days ago to Doctor Carstairs." (Thirty years ago Carstairs, of Baltimore, was the leading alienist in the country.) "He is coming tomorrow morning; but last night my husband was so restless that I sent for you today." Her rich voice, vibrating with suppressed feeling, made me think of stained glass windows and low organ music.

"Before we go in," I asked, "will you tell me as much as you can?"

Instead of replying to my request, she turned and laid her hand on the boy's shoulder. "Take the chips to Aunt Agatha, Benjamin," she said, "and tell her that the doctor has come."

While the child picked up the basket and ran up the sunken steps to the door, she watched him with breathless anxiety. Not until he had disappeared into the hall did she lift her eyes to my face again. Then, without answering my question, she murmured, with a sigh which was like the voice of that autumn evening, "We were once happy here." She was trying, I realized, to steel her heart against the despair that threatened it.

My gaze swept the obscure horizon, and returned to the moldering woodpile where we were standing. The yellow-green had faded from the sky, and the only light came from the house where a few scattered lamps were burning. Through the open door I could see the hall, as bare as if the house were empty, and the spiral staircase which crawled to the upper story. A fine old place once, but repulsive now in its abject decay, like some young blood of former days who has grown senile.

"Have you managed to wring a living out of the land?" I asked, because I could think of no words that were less compassionate.

"At first a poor one," she answered slowly. "We worked hard to keep things together, but we were happy. Then three years ago this illness came, and after that everything went against us. In the beginning it was simply brooding, a kind of melancholy, and we tried to ward it off by pretending that it was not real, that we imagined it. Only of late, when it became so much worse, have we admitted the truth, have we faced the reality——"

This passionate murmur, which had almost the effect of a chant rising out of the loneliness, was addressed, not to me, but to some abstract and implacable power. While she uttered it her composure was like the tranquillity of the dead. She did not lift her hand to hold her shawl, which was slipping unnoticed from her shoulders, and her eyes, so like dark flowers in their softness, did not leave my face.

"If you will tell me all, perhaps I may be able to help you," I said.

"But you know our story," she responded. "You must have heard it."

"Then it is true? Heredity, intermarriage, insanity?"

She did not wince at the bluntness of my speech. "My husband's grandfather is in an asylum, still living after almost thirty years. His father—my husband's, I mean—died there a few years ago. Two of his uncles are there. When it began I don't know, or how far back it reaches. We have never talked of it. We have tried always to forget it—— Even now I cannot put the thing into words—— My husband's mother died of a broken heart, but the grandmother and the two others are still living. You will see them when you go into the house. They are old women now, and they feel nothing."

"And there have been other cases?"

"I do not know. Are not four enough?"

"Do you know if it has assumed always the same form?" I was trying to be as brief as I could.

She flinched, and I saw that her unnatural calm was shaken at last. "The same, I believe. In the beginning there is melancholy, moping, Grandmother calls it, and then——" She flung out her arms with a despairing gesture, and I was reminded again of some tragic figure of legend.

"I know, I know," I was young, and in spite of my pride, my voice trembled. "Has there been in any case partial recovery, recurring at intervals?"

"In his grandfather's case, yes. In the others none. With them it has been hopeless from the beginning."

"And Carstairs is coming?"

"In the morning. I should have waited, but last night——" Her voice broke, and she drew the tattered shawl about her with a shiver. "Last night something happened. Something happened," she repeated, and could not go on. Then, collecting her strength with an effort which made her tremble like a blade of grass in the wind, she continued more quietly, "Today he has been better. For the first time he has slept, and I have been able to leave him. Two of the hands from the fields are in the room." Her tone changed suddenly, and a note of energy passed into it. Some obscure resolution brought a tinge of color to her pale cheek. "I must know," she added, "if this is as hopeless as all the others."

I took a step toward the house. "Carstairs's opinion is worth as much as that of any man living," I answered.

"But will he tell me the truth?"

I shook my head. "He will tell you what he thinks. No man's judgment is infallible."

Turning away from me, she moved with an energetic step to the house. As I followed her into the hall the threshold creaked under my tread, and I was visited by an apprehension, or, if you prefer, by a superstitious dread of the floor above. Oh, I got over that kind of thing before I was many years older; though in the end I gave up medicine, you know, and turned to literature as a safer outlet for a suppressed imagination.

But the dread was there at that moment, and it was not lessened by the glimpse I caught, at the foot of the spiral staircase, of a scantily furnished room, where three lean black-robed figures, as impassive as the Fates, were grouped in front of a wood fire. They were doing something with their hands. Knitting, crocheting, or plaiting straw?

At the head of the stairs the woman stopped and looked back at me. The light from the kerosene lamp on the wall fell over her, and I was struck afresh not only by the alien splendor of her beauty, but even more by the look of consecration, of impassioned fidelity that illumined her face.

"He is very strong," she said in a whisper. "Until this trouble came on him he had never had a day's illness in his life. We hoped that hard work, not having time to brood, might save us; but it has only brought the thing we feared sooner."

There was a question in her eyes, and I responded in the

same subdued tone. "His health, you say, is good?" What else was there for me to ask when I understood everything?

A shudder ran through her frame. "We used to think that a blessing, but now——" She broke off and then added in a lifeless voice, "We keep two field hands in the room day and night, lest one should forget to watch the fire, or fall asleep."

A sound came from a room at the end of the hall, and, without finishing her sentence, she moved swiftly toward the closed door. The apprehension, the dread, or whatever you choose to call it, was so strong upon me, that I was seized by an impulse to turn and retreat down the spiral staircase. Yes, I know why some men turn cowards in battle.

"I have come back, Alan," she said in a voice that wrung my heartstrings.

The room was dimly lighted; and for a minute after I entered, I could see nothing clearly except the ruddy glow of the wood fire in front of which two negroes were seated on low wooden stools. They had kindly faces, these men; there was a primitive humanity in their features, which might have been modelled out of the dark earth of the fields.

Looking round the next minute, I saw that a young man was sitting away from the fire, huddled over in a cretonne-covered chair with a high back and deep wings. At our entrance the negroes glanced up with surprise; but the man in the winged chair neither lifted his head nor turned his eyes in our direction. He sat there, lost within the impenetrable wilderness of the insane, as remote from us and from the sound of our voices as if he were the inhabitant of an invisible world. His head was sunk forward; his eyes were staring fixedly at some image we could not see; his fingers, moving restlessly, were plaiting and unplaiting the fringe of a plaid shawl. Distraught as he was, he still possessed the dignity of mere physical perfection. At his full height he must have measured not under six feet three; his hair was the color of ripe wheat, and his eyes, in spite of their fixed gaze, were as blue as the sky after rain. And this was only the beginning, I realized. With that constitution, that physical frame, he might live to be ninety.

"Alan!" breathed his wife again in her pleading murmur.

If he heard her voice, he gave no sign of it. Only when she crossed the room and bent over his chair, he put out his hand, with a gesture of irritation, and pushed her away, as if she were a veil of smoke which came between him and the object at which he was looking. Then his hand fell back to its old place, and he resumed his mechanical plaiting of the fringe.

The woman lifted her eyes to mine. "His father did that for twenty years," she said in a whisper that was scarcely more than a sigh of anguish.

When I had made my brief examination, we left the room as we had come, and descended the stairs together. The three old women were still sitting in front of the wood fire. I do not think they had moved since we went upstairs; but, as we reached the hall below, one of them, the youngest, I imagine, rose from her chair, and came out to join us. She was crocheting something soft and small, an infant's sack,[1] I perceived as she approached, of pink wool. The ball had rolled from her lap as she stood up, and it trailed after her now, like a woolen rose, on the bare floor. When the skein pulled at her, she turned back and stooped to pick up the ball, which she rewound with caressing fingers. Good God, an infant's sack in that house!

"Is it the same thing?" she asked.

"Hush!" responded the younger woman kindly. Turning to me she added, "We cannot talk here," and opening the door, passed out on the porch. Not until we had reached the lawn, and walked in silence to where my buggy stood beneath an old locust tree, did she speak again.

Then she said only, "You know now?"

"Yes, I know," I replied, averting my eyes from her face while I gave my directions as briefly as I could. "I will leave an opiate," I said. "Tomorrow, if Carstairs should not come, send for me again. If he does come," I added, "I will talk to him and see you afterward."

"Thank you," she answered gently; and taking the bottle from my hand, she turned away and walked quickly back to the house.

I watched her as long as I could; and then getting into my buggy, I turned my mare's head toward the woods, and drove by moonlight, past Buzzard's Tree and over the Old Stage Road, to my home. "I will see Carstairs tomorrow," was my last thought that night before I slept.

But, after all, I saw Carstairs only for a minute as he was taking the train. Life at its beginning and its end had filled my morning; and when at last I reached the little station, Carstairs had paid his visit, and was waiting on the platform for the approaching express. At first he showed a disposition to question me about the shooting, but as soon as I was able to make my errand clear, his jovial face clouded.

1. **sack:** A baby's jacket.

"So you've been there?" he said. "They didn't tell me. An interesting case, if it were not for that poor woman. Incurable, I'm afraid, when you consider the predisposing causes. The race is pretty well deteriorated, I suppose. God! what isolation! I've advised her to send him away. There are three others, they tell me, at Staunton."

The train came; he jumped on it, and was whisked away while I gazed after him. After all, I was none the wiser because of the great reputation of Carstairs.

All that day I heard nothing more from Jordan's End; and then, early next morning, the same negro brought me a message.

"Young Miss, she tole me ter ax you ter come along wid me jes' ez soon ez you kin git ready."

"I'll start at once, Uncle, and I'll take you with me."

My mare and buggy stood at the door. All I needed to do was to put on my overcoat, pick up my hat, and leave word, for a possible patient, that I should return before noon. I knew the road now, and I told myself, as I set out, that I would make as quick a trip as I could. For two nights I had been haunted by the memory of that man in the armchair, plaiting and unplaiting the fringe of the plaid shawl. And his father had done that, the woman had told me, for twenty years!

It was a brown autumn morning, raw, windless, with an overcast sky and a peculiar illusion of nearness about the distance. A high wind had blown all night, but at dawn it had dropped suddenly, and now there was not so much as a ripple in the broomsedge. Over the fields, when we came out of the woods, the thin trails of blue smoke were as motionless as cobwebs. The lawn surrounding the house looked smaller than it had appeared to me in the twilight, as if the barren fields had drawn closer since my last visit. Under the trees, where the few sheep were browsing, the piles of leaves lay in windrifts along the sunken walk and against the wings of the house.

When I knocked the door was opened immediately by one of the old women, who held a streamer of black cloth or rusty crepe[2] in her hands.

"You may go straight upstairs," she croaked; and, without waiting for an explanation, I entered the hall quickly, and ran up the stairs.

The door of the room was closed, and I opened it noiselessly, and stepped over the threshold. My first sensation, as I entered,

2. crepe: Thin crinkled cloth, often worn as a band around the arm, as a sign of mourning.

was one of cold. Then I saw that the windows were wide open, and that the room seemed to be full of people, though, as I made out presently, there was no one there except Alan Jordan's wife, her little son, the two old aunts, and an aged negress. On the bed there was something under a yellowed sheet of fine linen, which had been handed down from some more affluent generation.

When I went over, after a minute, and turned down one corner of the covering, I saw that my patient of the other evening was dead. Not a line of pain marred his features, not a thread of gray dimmed the wheaten gold of his hair. So he must have looked, I thought, when she first loved him. He had gone from life, not old, enfeebled and repulsive, but enveloped still in the romantic illusion of their passion.

As I entered, the two old women, who had been fussing about the bed, drew back to make way for me, but the negress did not pause in the weird chant, an incantation of some sort, which she was mumbling. From the rag carpet in front of the empty fireplace, the boy, with his father's hair and his mother's eyes, gazed at me silently, broodingly, as if I were trespassing; and by the open window, with her eyes on the ashen November day, the young wife stood as motionless as a statue. While I looked at her a redbird flew out of the boughs of a cedar, and she followed it with her eyes.

"You sent for me?" I said to her.

She did not turn. She was beyond the reach of my voice, of any voice, I imagine; but one of the palsied old women answered my question.

"He was like this when we found him this morning," she said. "He had a bad night, and Judith and the two hands were up with him until daybreak. Then he seemed to fall asleep, and Judith sent the hands, turn about, to get their breakfast."

While she spoke my eyes were on the bottle I had left there. Two nights ago it had been full, and now it stood empty, without a cork, on the mantelpiece. They had not even thrown it away. It was typical of the pervading inertia of the place that the bottle should still be standing there awaiting my visit.

For an instant the shock held me speechless; when at last I found my voice it was to ask mechanically.

"When did it happen?"

The old woman who had spoken took up the story. "Nobody knows. We have not touched him. No one but Judith has gone near him." Her words trailed off into unintelligible muttering. If she had ever had her wits about her, I dare-say fifty years at Jordan's End had unsettled them completely.

I turned to the woman at the window. Against the gray sky and the black intersecting branches of the cedar, her head, with its austere perfection, was surrounded by that visionary air of legend. So Antigone might have looked on the day of her sacrifice, I reflected. I had never seen a creature who appeared so withdrawn, so detached, from all human associations. It was as if some spiritual isolation divided her from her kind.

"I can do nothing," I said.

For the first time she looked at me, and her eyes were unfathomable. "No, you can do nothing," she answered. "He is safely dead."

The negress was still crooning on; the other old women were fussing helplessly. It was impossible in their presence, I felt, to put in words the thing I had to say.

"Will you come downstairs with me?" I asked. "Outside of this house?"

Turning quietly, she spoke to the boy. "Run out and play, dear. He would have wished it."

Then, without a glance toward the bed, or the old women gathered about it, she followed me over the threshold, down the stairs, and out on the deserted lawn. The ashen day could not touch her, I saw then. She was either so remote from it, or so completely a part of it, that she was impervious to its sadness. Her white face did not become more pallid as the light struck it; her tragic eyes did not grow deeper; her frail figure under the thin shawl did not shiver in the raw air. She felt nothing, I realized suddenly.

Wrapped in that silence as in a cloak, she walked across the windrifts of leaves to where my mare was waiting. Her step was so slow, so unhurried, that I remember thinking she moved like one who had all eternity before her. Oh, one has strange impressions, you know, at such moments!

In the middle of the lawn, where the trees had been stripped bare in the night, and the leaves were piled in long mounds like double graves, she stopped and looked in my face. The air was so still that the whole place might have been in a trance or asleep. Not a branch moved, not a leaf rustled on the ground, not a sparrow twittered in the ivy; and even the few sheep stood motionless, as if they were under a spell. Farther away, beyond the sea of broomsedge, where no wind stirred, I saw the flat desolation of the landscape. Nothing moved on the earth, but high above, under the leaden clouds, a buzzard was sailing.

I moistened my lips before I spoke. "God knows I want to help you!" At the back of my brain a hideous question was drumming. How had it happened? Could she have killed him? Had that delicate creature nerved her will to the unspeakable act? It was incredible. It was inconceivable. And yet. . . .

"The worst is over," she answered quietly, with that tearless agony which is so much more terrible than any outburst of grief. "Whatever happens, I can never go through the worst again. Once in the beginning he wanted to die. His great fear was that he might live too long, until it was too late to save himself. I made him wait then. I held him back by a promise."

So she had killed him, I thought. Then she went on steadily, after a minute, and I doubted again.

"Thank God, it was easier for him than he feared it would be," she murmured.

No, it was not conceivable. He must have bribed one of the negroes. But who had stood by and watched without intercepting? Who had been in the room? Well, either way! "I will do all I can to help you," I said.

Her gaze did not waver. "There is so little that any one can do now," she responded, as if she had not understood what I meant. Suddenly, without the warning of a sob, a cry of despair went out of her, as if it were torn from her breast. "He was my life," she cried, "and I must go on!"

So full of agony was the sound that it seemed to pass like a gust of wind over the broomsedge. I waited until the emptiness had opened and closed over it. Then I asked as quietly as I could:

"What will you do now?"

She collected herself with a shudder of pain. "As long as the old people live, I am tied here. I must bear it out to the end. When they die, I shall go away and find work. I am sending my boy to school. Doctor Carstairs will look after him, and he will help me when the time comes. While my boy needs me, there is no release."

While I listened to her, I knew that the question on my lips would never be uttered. I should always remain ignorant of the truth. The thing I feared most, standing there alone with her, was that some accident might solve the mystery before I could escape. My eyes left her face and wandered over the dead leaves at our feet. No, I had nothing to ask her.

"Shall I come again?" That was all.

She shook her head. "Not unless I send for you. If I need you, I will send for you," she answered; but in my heart I knew that she would never send for me.

I held out my hand, but she did not take it; and I felt that she meant me to understand, by her refusal, that she was beyond all consolation and all companionship. She was nearer to the bleak sky and the deserted fields than she was to her kind.

As she turned away, the shawl slipped from her shoulders to the dead leaves over which she was walking; but she did not stoop to recover it, nor did I make a movement to follow her. Long after she had entered the house I stood there, gazing down on the garment that she had dropped. Then climbing into my buggy, I drove slowly across the field and into the woods.

from

The Narrative of William Wells Brown, A Fugitive Slave

William Wells Brown

AT last the time for action arrived. The boat landed at a point which appeared to me the place of all others to start from. I found that it would be impossible to carry anything with me but what was upon my person. I had some provisions, and a single suit of clothes, about half worn. When the boat was discharging her cargo, and the passengers engaged carrying their baggage on and off shore, I improved the opportunity to convey myself with my little effects on land. Taking up a trunk, I went up the wharf, and was soon out of the crowd. I made directly for the woods, where I remained until night, knowing well that I could not travel, even in the state of Ohio, during the day, without danger of being arrested.

I had long since made up my mind that I would not trust myself in the hands of any man, white or colored. The slave is brought up to look upon every white man as an enemy to him and his race; and twenty-one years in slavery had taught me that there were traitors, even among colored people. After dark, I emerged from the woods into a narrow path, which led me into the main travelled road. But I knew not which way to go. I did not know north from south, east from west. I looked in vain for the North Star; a heavy cloud hid it from my view. I walked up and down the road until near midnight, when the clouds disappeared, and I welcomed the sight of my friend—truly the slave's friend—the North Star!

As soon as I saw it, I knew my course, and before daylight I travelled twenty or twenty-five miles. It being in the winter, I suffered intensely from the cold; being without an overcoat, and my other clothes rather thin for the season. I was provided with a tinder-box, so that I could make up a fire when necessary. And but for this, I should certainly have frozen to death; for I was determined not to go to any house for shelter. I knew of a man belonging to Gen. Ashly, of St. Louis, who had run away near Cincinnati, on the way to Washington, but had been caught and carried back into slavery; and I felt that a similar fate awaited me, should I be seen by any one. I travelled at night, and lay by during the day.

On the fourth day my provisions gave out, and then what to do I could not tell. Have something to eat I must; but how to get it was the question! On the first night after my food was gone, I went to a barn on the road-side and there found some ears of corn. I took ten or twelve of them, and kept on my journey. During the next day, while in the woods, I roasted my corn and feasted upon it, thanking God that I was so well provided for.

My escape to a land of freedom now appeared certain, and the prospects of the future occupied a great part of my thoughts. What should be my occupation, was a subject of much anxiety to me; and the next thing what should be my name? I have before stated that my old master, Dr. Young, had no children of his own, but had with him a nephew, the son of his brother, Benjamin Young. When this boy was brought to Dr. Young, his name being William, the same as mine, my mother was ordered to change mine to something else. This, at the time, I thought to be one of the most cruel acts that could be committed upon my rights; and I received several very severe whippings for telling people that my name was William, after orders were given to change it. Though young, I was old enough to place a high appreciation upon my name. It was decided, however, to call me "Sandford," and this name I was known by, not only upon my master's plantation, but up to the time that I made my escape. I was sold under the name of Sandford.

But as soon as the subject came to my mind, I resolved on adopting my old name of William, and let Sandford go by the board, for I always hated it. Not because there was anything peculiar in the name; but because it had been forced upon me. It is sometimes common, at the south, for slaves to take the name of their masters. Some have a legitimate right to do so. But I always detested the idea of being called by the name of either of my masters. And as for my father, I would rather have adopted the name of "Friday," and been known as the servant of some Robinson Crusoe, than to have taken his name. So I was not only hunting for my liberty, but also hunting for a name; though I regarded the latter as of little consequence, if I could but gain the former. Travelling along the road, I would sometimes speak to myself, sounding my name over, by way of getting used to it, before I should arrive among civilized human beings. On the fifth or sixth day, it rained very fast, and froze about as fast as it fell, so that my clothes were one glare of ice. I travelled on at night until I became so chilled and benumbed—the wind blowing into my face—that I found it impossible to go any further, and accordingly took shelter in a barn, where I was obliged to walk about to keep from freezing.

I have ever looked upon that night as the most eventful part of my escape from slavery. Nothing but the providence of God, and that old barn, saved me from freezing to death. I received a very severe cold, which settled upon my lungs, and from time to time my feet had been frostbitten, so that it was with difficulty I could walk. In this situation I travelled two days, when I found that I must seek shelter somewhere, or die.

The thought of death was nothing frightful to me, compared with that of being caught, and again carried back into slavery. Nothing but the prospect of enjoying liberty could have induced me to undergo such trials, for

> "Behind I left the whips and chains,
> Before me were sweet Freedom's plains!"

This, and this alone, cheered me onward. But I at last resolved to seek protection from the inclemency of the weather, and therefore I secured myself behind some logs and brush, intending to wait there until someone should pass by; for I thought it probable that I might see some colored person, or, if not, someone who was not a slave-holder; for I had an idea that I should know a slave-holder as far as I could see him.

The first person that passed was a man in a buggy-wagon. He looked too genteel for me to hail him. Very soon another passed by on horseback. I attempted to speak to him, but fear made my voice fail me. As he passed, I left my hidingplace and was approaching the road, when I observed an old man walking towards me, leading a white horse. He had on a broad-brimmed hat and a very long coat, and was evidently walking for exercise. As soon as I saw him, and observed his dress, I thought to myself, "You are the man that I have been looking for!" Nor was I mistaken. He was the very man!

On approaching me, he asked me, "if I was not a slave." I looked at him some time, and then asked him "if he knew of any one who would help me, as I was sick." He answered that he would; but again asked, if I was not a slave. I told him I was. He then said that I was in a very pro-slavery neighborhood, and if I would wait until he went home, he would get a covered wagon for me. I promised to remain. He mounted his horse, and was soon out of sight.

After he was gone, I meditated whether to wait or not; being apprehensive that he had gone for someone to arrest me. But I finally concluded to remain until he should return; removing some few rods to watch his movements. After a suspense of an hour and a half or more, he returned with a two-horse covered wagon, such as are usually seen under the shed of a Quaker meetinghouse on Sundays and Thursdays; for the old man proved to be a Quaker of the George Fox stamp.[1]

He took me to his house, but it was some time before I could be induced to enter it; not until the old lady came out, did I venture into the house. I thought I saw something in the old lady's cap that told me I was not only safe, welcome, in her house. I was not, however, prepared to receive their hospitalities. The only fault I found with them was their being too kind. I had never had a white man treat me as an equal, and the idea of a white lady waiting on me at the table was still worse! Though the table was loaded with the good things of this life, I could not eat. I thought if I could only be allowed the privilege of eating in the kitchen I should be more than satisfied!

Finding that I could not eat, the old lady, who was a "Thompsonian,"[2] made me a cup of "composition," or "number six;" but it was so strong and hot, that I called it *"number seven!"* However, I soon found myself at home in this family. On different occasions, when telling these facts, I have been asked how I felt upon finding myself regarded as a man by a white family; especially just having run away from one. I cannot say that I have ever answered the question yet.

The fact that I was in all probability a freeman, sounded in my ears like a charm. I am satisfied that none but a slave could place such an appreciation upon liberty as I did at that time. I wanted to see mother and sister, that I might tell them "I was free!" I wanted to see my fellow-slaves in St. Louis, and let them know that the chains were no longer upon my limbs. I wanted to see Captain Price, and let him learn from my own lips that I was no more a chattel, but a man! I was anxious, too, thus to inform Mrs. Price that she must get another coachman. And I

1. **George Fox Stamp:** George Fox (1624–1691), founder of the Society of Friends (Quakers) in England in 1650. The Quakers, both as an organized body and individually, were known as opponents to slavery.
2. **Thompsonian:** A system of medicine named for Samuel Thompson (1769–1843) who advocated the exclusive use of vegetable drugs in treating disease.

wanted to see Eliza more than I did either Mr. or Mrs. Price!

The fact that I was a freeman—could walk, talk, eat and sleep, as a man, and no one to stand over me with the blood-clotted cow-hide—all this made me feel that I was not myself.

The kind friend that had taken me in was named Wells Brown. He was a devoted friend of the slave; but was very old, and not in the enjoyment of good health. After being by the fire awhile, I found that my feet had been very much frozen. I was seized with a fever, which threatened to confine me to my bed. But my Thompsonian friends soon raised me, treating me as kindly as if I had been one of their own children. I remained with them twelve or fifteen days, during which time they made me some clothing, and the old gentleman purchased me a pair of boots.

I found that I was about fifty or sixty miles from Dayton, in the State of Ohio, and between one and two hundred miles from Cleveland, on Lake Erie, a place I was desirous of reaching on my way to Canada. This I know will sound strangely to the ears of people in foreign lands, but it is nevertheless true. An American citizen was fleeing from a democratic, republican, government, to receive protection under the monarchy of Great Britain. While the people of the United States boast of their freedom, they at the same time keep three millions of their own citizens in chains; and while I am seated here in sight of Bunker Hill Monument, writing this narrative, I am a slave, and no law, not even in Massachusetts, can protect me from the hands of the slave-holder!

Before leaving this good Quaker friend, he inquired what my name was besides William. I told him that I had no other name. "Well," said he, "thee must have another name. Since thee has got out of slavery, thee has become a man, and men always have two names."

I told him that he was the first man to extend the hand of friendship to me, and I would give him the privilege of naming me.

"If I name thee," said he, "I shall call thee Wells Brown, after myself."

"But," said I, "I am not willing to lose my name of William. As it was taken from me once against my will, I am not willing to part with it again upon any terms."

"Then," said he, "I will call thee William Wells Brown."

"So be it," said I; and I have been known by that name ever since I left the house of my first white friend, Wells Brown.

After giving me some little change, I again started for Canada. In four days I reached a public house, and went in to warm myself. I there learned that some fugitive slaves had just passed through the place. The men in the bar-room were talking about it, and I thought that it must have been myself they referred to, and I was therefore afraid to start, fearing they would seize me; but I finally mustered courage enough, and took my leave. As soon as I was out of sight, I went into the woods, and remained there until night, when I again regained the road, and travelled on until next day.

Not having had any food for nearly two days, I was faint with hunger, and was in a dilemma what to do, as the little cash supplied me by my adopted father, and which had contributed to my comfort, was now all gone. I however concluded to go to a farm-house, and ask for something to eat. On approaching the door of the first one presenting itself, I knocked, and was soon met by a man who asked me what I wanted. I told him that I would like something to eat. He asked me where I was from, and where I was going. I replied that I had come some way, and was going to Cleveland.

After hesitating a moment or two, he told me that he could give me nothing to eat, adding, "that if I would work, I could get something to eat."

I felt bad, being thus refused something to sustain nature, but did not dare tell him that I was a slave.

Just as I was leaving the door, with a heavy heart, a woman, who proved to be the wife of this gentleman, came to the door, and asked her husband what I wanted. He did not seem inclined to inform her. She therefore asked me herself. I told her that I had asked for something to eat. After a few other questions, she told me to come in, and that she would give me something to eat.

I walked up to the door, but the husband remained in the passage, as if unwilling to let me enter.

She asked him two or three times to get out of the way, and let me in. But as he did not move, she pushed him on one side, bidding me walk in! I was never before so glad to see a woman push a man aside!

After giving me as much food as I could eat, she presented me with ten cents, all the money then at her disposal, accompanied with a note to a friend, a few miles further on the road. Thanking this angel of mercy from an overflowing heart, I pushed on my way, and in three days arrived at Cleveland, Ohio.

Being an entire stranger in this place, it was difficult for me to find where to stop. I had no money, and the lake being frozen, I saw that I must remain until the opening of the navigation, or go to Canada by way of Buffalo. But believing myself to be somewhat out of danger, I secured an engagement at the

Mansion House, as a table waiter, in payment for my board. The proprietor, however, whose name was E. M. Segur, in a short time, hired me for twelve dollars a month; on which terms I remained until spring, when I found good employment on board a lake steamboat.

I purchased some books, and at leisure moments perused them with considerable advantage to myself. While at Cleveland, I saw, for the first time, an anti-slavery newspaper. It was the *"Genius of Universal Emancipation,"* published by Benjamin Lundy; and though I had no home, I subscribed for the paper. It was my great desire, being out of slavery myself, to do what I could for the emancipation of my brethren yet in chains, and while on Lake Erie, I found many opportunities of "helping their cause along."

It is well known that a great number of fugitives make their escape to Canada, by way of Cleveland; and while on the lakes, I always made arrangement to carry them on the boat to Buffalo or Detroit, and thus effect their escape to the "promised land." The friends of the slave, knowing that I would transport them without charge, never failed to have a delegation when the boat arrived at Cleveland. I have sometimes had four or five on board at one time.

In the year 1842, I conveyed, from the first of May to the first of December, sixty-nine fugitives over Lake Erie to Canada. In 1843, I visited Malden, in Upper Canada, and counted seventeen in that small village, whom I had assisted in reaching Canada. Soon after coming north I subscribed for the Liberator, edited by that champion of freedom, William Lloyd Garrison.[3] I had heard nothing of the anti-slavery movement while in slavery, and as soon as I found that my enslaved countrymen had friends who were laboring for their liberation, I felt anxious to join them, and give what aid I could to the cause.

I early embraced the temperance cause, and found that a temperance reformation was needed among my colored brethren. In company with a few friends, I commenced a temperance reformation among the colored people in the city of Buffalo, and labored three years, in which time a society was built up, numbering over five hundred out of a population of less than seven hundred.

In the autumn, 1843, impressed with the importance of spreading anti-slavery truth, as a means to bring about the abolition of slavery, I commenced lecturing as an agent of the western New York Anti-Slavery Society, and have ever since devoted my time to the cause of my enslaved countrymen.

3. William Lloyd Garrison: (1805–1879), U.S. editor, lecturer, and abolitionist leader.

from

In Abraham's Bosom

Paul Green

Abraham McCranie is the son of an African American woman and her former white master, Colonel McCranie, a North Carolina plantation owner. Abraham's education and experience are limited, but he dreams of wider opportunities for himself and others. For this reason, he attempts to establish a school to provide education for African Americans. In this excerpt from Scene i of the play, we see Abraham's love of learning and hatred of ignorance—and his determination to found a school despite opposition from a conservative society. The excerpt ends with the situation unresolved.

BUD. Them books he got to studying last year or two. Can't go to the woods without 'em. Look up there on his bucket, for cripes sake. *(He points to the remaining tin bucket in the bush. A small book is lying on the top under the handle. He snorts.)* 'Rifmatic, I bet.

PUNY. *(pouring molasses on his bread)* He smart enough, though, in his head. That buddy got sense.

LIJE. Has that. Getting so he can cipher[1] right up with the Colonel.

PUNY. *(looking at* BUD*)* Bet some day Colonel Mack put him woods boss over us.

BUD. Ain't no black man gwine boss me, old son.

LIJE. *(leaning back and emitting a halloo)* Heigh!, you Abel Dinner! Gwine cut all day?

BUD. Give him the full title and he'll hear you.

LIJE. *(grinning)* Aberham, Aberham McCranie!

PUNY. Yeh, you Aberham Lincoln, you better get your grub!

An answering shout comes out of the forest.

1. **cipher:** To solve arithmetic problems.

BUD. Trying to cut past time—maybe us'll think he's smart.

PUNY. Don't care what you think, Bud, getting so he look down on you and the rest of us.

BUD. Your runty soul, what you know about it? Ain't no black man living can look down on me and get by with it. Do, and I make him smell of that. *(He clenches his heavy fist and raises it to heaven.)*

PUNY. Jesus! That Abe take you up in one hand and frail your behind to a blister.

LIJE. What make you two blackguard[2] so much?

BUD. *(to* PUNY*)* Keep on, keep on, little man. Some these days you gwine come missing. *(He crams a handful of corn bread into his mouth.)*

LIJE. *(drawling).* Try a little fist and skull and work the bile out'n your systems. *(Looking off and singing.)*

Dark was the night and cold the ground——

BUD. *(spitting in scorn).* Ain't gwine bruise my fists on his old skull. Don't 'spect to notice him no more. *(He falls to eating in huge mouthfuls.)* But he better quit throwing that Abe in my face, I tells him that.

PUNY. Don't see why that make you mad.

BUD. It do though. I don't like him and his uppity ways, I don't.

PUNY. Hunh, and you was one of the first to brag on him for going on short rations so the Colonel buy him books and learn him to teach school.

BUD. Short rations. Ain't no short rations, and that Goldie gal bringing him pies and stuff every day. Be here with a bucket in a few minutes, I betcha. Fool love the very ground he squat on! And he look down on her 'cause her ignorant. And teach school! Been hearing that school-teaching business the whole year. He ain't gwine teach no school. Colored folks won't send to him, they won't. They don't want no schooling.

PUNY. Might. Abe told me this morning that the Colonel gwine fix it with the commissioners or something in town today. I know what the matter with you, Bud. Hee-hee.

2. **blackguard:** To verbally abuse a person.

BUD. What?

PUNY. *(hesitating)* Abe come riding by in two-horse coach. Us'll be bowing and a-scraping. Us'll pull off our hats and be "Howdy, Mister Aberham." *(*BUD *turns and looks at him with infinite scorn, saying nothing.)* And Bud? *(*BUD *makes no answer.)* Bud?

BUD. What?

PUNY. That Goldie business what worrying you, hee-hee. She love Abe and—

BUD. *(bounding up and kicking* PUNY's *bucket and food into the bushes)* Damn your lousy soul, I'm a mind to stomp you in the dirt! *(He towers over the terrified* PUNY, *who lies flat on his back whimpering.)*

PUNY. Don't hit me, Bud. For God's sake! I just joking.

LIJE. Go at it, fight it out. *(Singing to his inner self as he watches them.)*

The bones in the grave cried Calvary
The night King Jesus died.

BUD. *(kicking dirt at* PUNY *and going back to his bucket)* Done told him now. Ain't gwine say no more! Next time be my fist rammed down his throat, and turn him wrong side outwards.

ABE *comes in at the right, carrying his ax. He is a young Negro, with a touch of the mulatto in him, of twenty-five or six, tall and powerfully built and dressed much like the others in cap and turpentine-glazed clothes. He puts his ax by the pine at the right, pulls off his cap and fans himself, while he pinches his sweaty shirt loose from his skin. His shaggy head, forehead, and jaw are marked with will and intelligence. But his wide nostril and a smoldering flash in his eye that now and then shows itself suggest a passionate and dangerous person when aroused. From the change in the actions of the others when he enters it is evident that they respect and even fear him.*

ABE. What's the trouble between you and Puny, Bud?

BUD. *(sullenly)* Ain't no trouble.

PUNY. *(crawling around on the ground and collecting his spilled food)* Ain't nothing, Abe, I just spilled my rations.

ABE *gets his book down and seats himself in the shade at the left. He begins working problems, using a stub of a pencil and a sheet of crumpled paper.*

LIJE. Puny, I got some bread left you can have. *(He pulls a mouth harp from his pocket and begins to blow softly.)*

PUNY. *(straightening out his mashed bucket and closing it)* I don't want nothing else, Lije. Et all I can hold. *(After a moment)* Put your bucket up for you.

He gets LIJE'S *bucket and hangs it along with his own in the limby bush.* BUD *eats in silence, puts up his bucket, gets a drink from the spring, and resumes his seat, hanging his head between his knees.* PUNY *goes to the spring and drinks.*

BUD. *(pouring snuff into his lip)* Don't fall in and get drownded, Puny.

PUNY. Want some water, Lije? *(He goes to the log, curls himself up in the shade beside it and prepares to sleep.)*

LIJE. *(stirring lazily)* Believe I does. *(He goes to the spring and drinks, returns to the pine tree and sits down.)*

PUNY. Ain't you gwine eat no dinner, Abe?

ABE *makes no reply.*

LIJE. Call him again. *(Touching his head with his finger)* Deep, deep up there.

PUNY. Heigh, Abe, better eat your grub.

ABE. *(starting)* You call me?

PUNY. You so deep studying didn't hear me. Better eat your dinner. Get full of ants setting up there.

ABE. I'm going to eat later.

BUD. Yeh, when Goldie come.

ABE. Hunh!

BUD. You heared me.

ABE. Don't let me hear no more.

BUD. Hunh!

ABE. You heard me. *(*PUNY *snickers from his log with audible* *delight.* LIJE *waits a moment and then lies down.* BUD *reaches out and tears a bush from the ground and casts it angrily from him.)* I'll eat my dinner when it pleases me, you gentlemen allowing. *(There is a touch of anger in his voice which he apparently regrets on second thought, for he goes on more kindly.)* Goldie said she's going to fetch me something to eat today. I got to work this problem. Been at it two days now. Can't get it out'n my head. Ain't been able to sleep for two nights. *(*BUD *sits staring and spitting straight before him. Presently* LIJE *begins to snore, then* PUNY *follows.* ABE *goes on with his figuring.* BUD *turns over on the ground and goes to sleep.* ABE *becomes more and more absorbed in the problem he is working. He mutters to himself.)* Answer say fifteen. Can't make it come out fifteen, can't, seem like, to save me. Must have answer wrong. Six go into fourteen, three, no, two times and—two over. *(His voice dies away as he becomes lost in his work. Presently his face begins to light up. He figures faster. Suddenly he slaps his knee.)* There where I been missing it all the time. I carried two instead of one. Blame fool I is. *(He hits the side of his head with his knuckle. In his excitement he calls out.)* Puny, I'm getting that answer. *(But* PUNY *is snoring away. In a moment* ABE *throws down his book with beaming face.)* I got it, folkses, I got it. Fifteen! *(He turns expectantly toward* LIJE.*)* I got it, Lije. *(*LIJE *makes no answer. He turns toward* PUNY *again, starts to speak, but sees he is asleep.)* Bud! *(But* BUD *makes no answer. The heavy breathing of the sleepers falls regularly upon his ears. His face sinks into a sort of hopeless brooding.)* Yeh, sleep, sleep, sleep your life away. I figger for you, for me, for all the black in the world to lead 'em up out of ignorance. They don't listen, they don't hear me, they in the wilderness, don't want to be led. They sleep, sleep in bondage. *(Presently.)* Time me to eat.

ABE *reaches for his bucket and is about to open it when* PUNY *springs high into the air with a squeak of terror and begins rolling over and over in the leaves and briers.*

PUNY. Come here, folkses, come here and get this thing off'n me.

PUNY *clutches at his breeches.* LIJE *and* BUD *start up out of their sleep.*

LIJE. Who that run-mad man?

BUD. That Puny, something in his britches!

ABE. Be still, Puny, I get it out. *(He goes up to the frightened* PUNY, *reaches down his trousers, and pulls out a mouse.)* Nothing but a little bitty old field mice.

ABE *throws the mouse into the thicket.* LIJE *and* BUD *break into roaring laughter.* PUNY *sits down exhausted, fanning himself angrily.*

PUNY. Laugh, laugh, all of you. That thing bite same as a mud turtle. Yeh, funny, funny.

PUNY *snaps his mouth closed and fans himself the more furiously. A loud shout comes from off the left.*

ABE. Stop your laughing, I hear somebody hollering.

A second halloo comes down the hill.

PUNY. That the Colonel and Mr. Lonnie!

BUD. Sound like 'em. That's who 'tis.

ABE. *(going off at the left)* Here we is, Colonel Mack, at the spring eating dinner! *(He comes back.)* Colonel Mack and Mr. Lonnie coming on down here.

PUNY. 'Course. Got to see how many boxes us cleaned up this morning.

ABE. He tell me about the school now. *(He stirs around him in his excitement.)* Mebbe that his main business here in the middle of the day.

BUD. Hunh, mebbe. Got some special work wants done. Wants to hurry us to it, that's what.

The sound of voices is heard approaching from the left, and almost immediately the COLONEL *and his son* LONNIE *come in. The* COLONEL *carries a riding whip. He is a stout run-down southerner, past middle age, with all the signs of moral and intellectual decadence upon him, and yet he has retained a kind of native good-naturedness. His shirt front and once pointed beard are stained with the drippings of tobacco juice. There is something in his bearing and in the contour of his face that resembles* ABE. *His son, a heavyish florid young man of twenty-three or four, walks behind him.*

COLONEL. *(in a high jerky voice)* Snoozing, hanh?

ABE. Just finishing our dinner, suh.

PUNY. Us about to work overtime today, Colonel.

COLONEL. Not likely, I reckon. Say, I want you fellows, all four of you, to get over to the swamp piece on Dry Creek. Boxes there are running over, two quarts in 'em apiece, prime virgin. *(They begin to move to their feet.)* No, I don't mean to go right now. Gabe's coming by on the big road here with a load of barrels and the dippers in about a half-hour. Meet him out there.

LONNIE. Yeh, we want to get the wagons off to Fayetteville tonight.

COLONEL. How you get on cornering this morning, Bud?

BUD. Purty good, suh. Us four done about all that pasture piece, suh.

COLONEL. Fine, fine. That's the way, Puny and Lije stay with you?

BUD. Right there every jump.

LIJE. Yes, suh, yes, suh!

PUNY. When he give the call we give him the response every time, suh. Yes, suh, us kept him crowded.

COLONEL. We got to get on, Lonnie. Want to see how the scrape's coming over on Uncle Joe's Branch. Be up on the road therein half an hour.

LONNIE. *(stopping as they go out)* Got so you doing any better work lately, Abe?

ABE. *(starting)* Suh?

LONNIE. You heard me.

ABE. I didn't understand you, Mr. Lonnie.

LONNIE. You understood me all right. *(Pointing to the book on the ground.)* Let them books worry you still?

COLONEL. Come on, Lonnie.

ABE. *(stammering)* I dunno—I——

COLONEL. Still holding out on short rations, ain't you, Abe? *(There is the least hint of pride in the* COLONEL'S *voice.)*

ABE. *(somewhat confused)* I studying what I can. Slow go, slow go.

COLONEL. Stick to it. You're the first Negro I ever saw so determined. But then you're uncommon! *(The* COLONEL *moves on.)* Come on, Lonnie.

ABE. *(following somewhat timidly after him)* Colonel Mack, did, di—you—what'd they say over there about that little school business?

COLONEL. Bless my soul, about to forget it. I talked it over with the board and most of 'em think maybe we'd better not try it yet.

ABE. *(his face falling)* When they say it might be a good time? I'm getting right along with that 'rithmetic and spelling and reading. I can teach the boys and girls a whole heap right now, and I'll keep studying.

COLONEL. *(impatiently)* Oh, I dunno. Time'll come maybe. Maybe time won't come. Folks are queer things, you know. *(He moves on.)*

On the Mountainside

Elizabeth Madox Roberts

THERE was a play-party at the schoolhouse at the bottom of the cove. Newt Reddix waited outside the house, listening to the noises as Lester Hunter, the teacher, had listened to them—a new way for Newt. Sound at the bottom of a cove was different from sound at the top, he noticed, for at the top voices spread into a wide thinness. Before Lester came, Newt had let his ears have their own way of listening. Sounds had then been for but one purpose—to tell him what was happening or what was being said. Now the what of happenings and sayings was wrapped about with some unrelated feeling or prettiness, or it stood back beyond some heightened qualities.

"Listen!" Lester had said to him one evening, standing outside a house where a party was going forward. "Listen!" And there were footsteps and outcries of men and women, happy cries, shrill notes of surprise and pretended anger, footsteps on rough wood, unequal intervals, a flare of fiddle playing and a tramp of dancing feet. Down in the cove the sounds from a party were different from those that came from a house on the side of a hill, the cries of men bent and disturbed, distorted by the place, by the sink and rise of land. While he listened, the knowledge that Lester Hunter would soon go out of the country, the school term being over, brought a loneliness to his thought.

He went inside the schoolhouse and flung his hat on the floor beside the door; he would take his part now in the playing. His hat was pinned up in front with a thorn and was as pert a hat as any of those beside the door, and no one would give it dishonor: The schoolteacher was stepping about in the dance, turning Corie Yancey, and the fiddle was scraping the top of a tune. For him the entire party was filled with the teacher's impending departure.

"Ladies change and gents the same," the fiddler called, his voice unblended with the tune he played. Newt fell into place when an older man withdrew in his favor and gave him Ollie Mack for his partner. The teacher danced easily, bent to the curve of the music, neglectful and willing, giving the music the flowing lightness of his limp body.

Newt wanted to dance as the teacher did, but he denied himself and kept the old harsh gesture, pounding the floor more roughly now and then with a deeply accented step. He wanted to tread the music lightly, meeting it halfway, but he would not openly imitate anybody. While he danced he was always, moment by moment, aware of the teacher, aware of him standing to wait his turn, pulling his collar straight, pushing his hands into the pockets of his coat, looking at Ollie Mack when she laughed, looking full into her face with pleasure, unafraid. The teacher had given an air to the dance, and had made it, for him, more bold in form, more like itself or more true to its kind, more gentle in courtesy. Lester had come from one of the low counties of the rolling plain where the curving creeks of the Pigeon River spread slowly, winding broadly, to gather up many little rills. Newt had learned somewhere, in his own blood, to hate the lower country for its pleasantness. There the fields rolled out smoothly and the soil was deep. The grass of any roadside was bluegrass mingled, perhaps, with rich weeds. Fat cattle, fine beasts, ate in the mythical pastures. Smooth roads ran between the farms. Dancing, shaking his body stiffly with the beat of the fiddle, Newt saw that Lester took his partner's hand lightly, that he gave equal courtesy to all the women, calling them ladies. He wanted to be as the teacher was, but he could not. The dance drawing to an end, he realized again that in two days more the teacher would go, for he had set his head upon some place far away, down in the settlements, among the lower counties from which he had come six months earlier.

There was pie for a treat, baked by Marthy Anne Sands and brought to the schoolhouse in a great hickory basket. Standing about eating the pie, all were quiet, regretting the teacher's going. Newt wove a vagrant path in and out among them, hearing the talk of the older men and women.

"My little tad, the least one, Becky, is plumb bereft over 'im," one said, a woman speaking.

"Last year at the school there wasn't hardly anybody would go, and look at this. I had to whop Joel to make him stay on the place one day to feed and water the property whilst I had to go. Hit appears like Joel loves book-sense since Les Hunter come up the mountain."

"What makes you in such a swivet to go nohow?" one asked.

"Did you come up the gorge to borrow fire you're in such a swivet to get on?"

"There's a big meeten over to Kitty's branch next light moon. Why don't you stay? No harm in you to be broguen about a small spell."

"You could loafer around a spell and wait for the meeten."

"Big meeten. And nohow the meeten needs youens to help sing."

"What's he in such a swivet to go off for?"

"I got to go. I got to see the other end of the world yet."

"What's he a-sayen?"

"I got to go to the other end of the world."

"That's too far a piece."

"That surely undoubtedly is a right smart piece to go."

"He could stay a spell at my place and welcome. I'd be real proud to have him stay with my folks a spell. And Nate, he'd keep youens a week, that I right well know. Youens could loafer around awhile as well as not."

"He always earns his way and more, ever since he kem up the mountain, always earns his keep, anyhow."

"I've got to go. I'm bound for the other end of this old globe. I'm obliged all the same, but I got a heap to see yet. I'm bound to go."

Newt plowed the corn in the rocky field above the house where he lived, one horse to the plow, or he hoed where the field lay steepest. The teacher was gone now. On Sunday Newt would put on his clean shirt his mother had washed on Friday, and climb up the gorge to the head of the rise and meet there Tige English and Jonathan Evans. Then they would go to see Lum Baker's girls. He would contrive to kiss each girl before the night fell and Lum would cry out: "Come on, you gals now, and milk the cow brutes." Or sometimes they would go down the way to see Corie Yancey and Ollie Mack. To Newt all the place seemed still since the teacher had left, idle, as if it had lost its uses and its future. Going to the well for water he would stare at the winch, at the soft rot of the bucket, at the stones inside the well curb, or he would listen intently to the sounds as the vessel struck the water or beat against the stones.

The noises gave him more than the mere report of a bucket falling into a well to get water; they gave him some comprehension of all things that were yet unknown. The sounds, rich with tonality, as the bucket struck the water, rang with some strange sonority and throbbed with a beat that was like something he could not define, some other, unlike fiddle playing but related to it in its unlikeness. A report had come to him from an outside world and a suspicion of more than he could know in his present state haunted him. He cried out inwardly for the answer, or he looked about him and listened, remembering all that he could of what Lester Hunter had taught—capitals of countries, seaports, buying and selling, nouns, verbs, numbers multiplied together to make other numbers. Now he looked intently and listened. He detected a throb in sound, but again there was a beat in the hot sun over a moist field. One day he thought that he had divined a throb in numbers as he counted, a beat in the recurrences of kinds, but this evaded him. He listened and looked at the well happenings, at the house wall, at the rail fence, at the barn, at the hills going upward toward the top of the gorge.

On every side were evasions. These sights and sounds could not give him enough; they lay flat against the air; they were imbedded within his own flesh and were sunk into his own sense of them. He would stare at the green and brown moss on the broken frame of the well box and stare again at the floating images in the dark of the well water. The rope would twine over the axle as he turned the wooden handle, and the rounds of the rope would fall into orderly place, side by side, as he knew too casually and too well. Since the teacher had gone the place had flattened to an intolerable staleness that gave out meager tokens of withheld qualities and beings—his mother leaning from the door to call him to dinner, his sister dragging his chair to the table and setting his cup beside his place, the old dog running out to bark at some varmint above in the brush. He could hardly separate the fall of his own bare foot from the rock doorstep over which he had walked since he could first walk at all. His thirst and his water to drink were one now. His loneliness, as he sat to rest at noon beside the fence, merged and was identified with the still country from brush-grown slope to brush-grown slope.

His father began to clear a new patch below the house; they grubbed at the roots all day when the corn was laid by. One morning in September, when the sun, moving south, was just getting free of Rattlesnake Hill, it came to him that he would go down to the settlements, that he would go to Merryman. All summer he had known that there was a school at Merryman, but he had not thought to go there, for he had no money. It came to him as a settled fact that he would go there and look about at the place. Three high ridges with numberless breaks and gorges intervened; he had heard this said by men who knew or had heard of what lay beyond. The determination to set forth and the wish to go came to him at one instant. "My aim, hit's to go there," he said. "I lay off to do that-there, like I say."

He remembered the teacher more clearly at this moment, saw him in a more sharply detailed picture; his own breath jerked deeply inward as he was himself related, through his intended departure, to the picture. Hunter was remembered cutting wood for the schoolhouse fire, sweethearting the girls and turning them lightly in the dance, or sitting by the fire at night, reading his book, holding the page low to the blaze. He was remembered hallooing back up the mountain the day he left, his voice calling back as he went down the ridge and he himself answering until there was not even a faint hollow whoopee to come up the slope. By the fire Newt had often taken Hunter's book into his hands, but he could never read the strange words nor in any way know what they meant when they were read, for they had stood four-square and hostile against his understanding. His father's voice would fall dully over the slow clearing: "You could work on this-here enduren the while that I cut the corn patch."

He knew that he would go. His determination rejected the clearing, knowing that he would be gone before the corn was ready to cut. It rejected the monotonous passing of the days, the clutter of feet on the stones by the door, the dull, inconspicuous corn patch above. He would walk, taking the short cut over the mountains. Two ridges to go and then there would be a road for his feet, someone had said. He announced his plan to his father one day while they leaned over their grub hoes. There was no willingness offered, but his mind was set, and three days later he had established his plan. His mother had washed his shirts clean and had rolled them into a bundle with his spare socks, and she had baked him bread and a joint of ham. She and his sister stood by the doorway weeping after he had driven back the dog and had shouted his goodbye.

It was a mid-afternoon and the sun beat down into the cove where he traveled. He worked his way through the thick-set laurel, struggling to keep his bundle tied to his shoulders where the brush stood most dense.

The dry clatter of the higher boughs came to his ears, but it was so mingled with the pricking snarls of the twigs on his face that the one sense was not divided from the other. "This durned ivy," he said when the laurel held him back. He matched his strength against boughs or he flashed his wits against snarls and rebounds, hot and weary, tingling with sweat and with the pricking twigs. Pushed back at one place where he tried to find an opening, he assailed another and then another, throwing all his strength angrily against the brush and tearing himself through the mesh. A large shaded stone that bulged angrily out of the mountainside gave him a space of rest. He stretched himself on the slanting rock, his face away from the sun, and lay for an hour, thinking nothing, feeling the weariness as it beat heavily upon his limbs.

"I'm bodaciously tired," he said, after a long period of torpor. "Could I come by a spring branch, I'd drink me a whole durned quart of it."

Another tree-grown mountain arose across the cove, misty now in the afternoon and in the first haze of autumn, and beyond lay other blue mountains, sinking farther and farther into the air. Back of him it was the same; he had been on the way two weeks now. Before him he knew each one would be dense with laurel until he came to the wagon road. He took to the pathless way after his hour of rest, going forward. When the sun was setting behind Bee Gum Mountain, he saw a house down in the cove, not far as the crow would fly but the distance of two hours' going for him. When he saw the cabin he began to sing, chanting:

Right hands across and howdy-do,
Left and back and how are you.

Oh, call up yo' dog, oh, call up yo' dog,
Ring twang a-whoddle lanky day.

The sight of the house quickened his desire for Merryman and the cities and counties in the settlements, and this desire had become more definite in his act of going. His wish was for sure, quick gestures and easy sayings that would come from the mouth as easily as breath. There were for him other things, as yet unrelated to any one place—men playing ball with a great crowd to watch, all the crowd breaking into a laugh at one time; men racing fine horses on a hard, smooth track; music playing; men having things done by machinery; lovely girls not yet imagined; and things to know beyond anything he could recall, and not one of them too fine or too good for him. He sang as he went down the slope, his song leaping out of him. He had heard it said that the lights of Merryman could be seen from Coster Ridge on a clear night, and Coster was now visible standing up in the pale air, for a man had pointed him the way that morning. Singing, he set himself toward the house at the bottom of the cove.

Night was falling when he called "Hello" at the foot of Bee Gum Mountain. The man of the house asked his name and told his own, making him welcome. Supper was over, but the host, whose name was Tom Bland, ordered Nance, his woman, to give the stranger a snack of biscuit bread and bacon, and this Newt ate sitting beside the fire. Another stranger was sitting in the cabin, an old man who kept very still while Nance worked with the utensils, his dim eyes looking into the fire or eyeing Newt, who stared back and searched the looks of the stranger. Then Tom told Nance how they would sleep that night, telling her to give the old man her place in the bed beside himself.

"You could get in bed along with the young ones," he said to her. "The boy here, he could sleep on a shakedown alongside the fireplace."

From gazing into the fire the old stranger would fall asleep, but after a moment he would awake, opening dim, ashamed eyes that glanced feebly at Newt, faintly defying him. Then Nance put some children to bed, her own perhaps, and sat quietly in the corner of the hearth, her hands in her lap. Newt had looked at the host, acquainting himself with him. He was a strong man, far past youth, large-boned and broad-muscled. His heavy feet scraped on the floor when he moved from his chair to the water bucket on the window sill. Newt saw that he on his side had been silently searching out the old stranger. After a while the host and the old man began to talk, Tom speaking first.

"There's a sight of travel now."

"Hit's a moven age."

Between each speech there was a slow pause as each saying was carefully probed before the reply was offered.

Tom said: "Two in one night, and last week there was one come by." And then after a while he asked: "Where might youens be bound for, stranger?"

"I'm on my way back," the man said.

There was a long season of quiet. The ideas were richly interspersed with action, for Nance softly jolted back and forth in her chair, her bare feet tapping lightly on the boards of the floor.

"You been far?" Tom asked.

"I been a right far piece. I been to the settlements in Froman county, and then I been to the mines around Tateville and Beemen."

Newt bit nervously at his knuckles and looked at the man, taking from him these signs of the world. The fire burned low, and breaking the long silence Tom said once or twice: "There's a sight of travel now." Newt looked at the old man's feet in their patched shoes, feet that had walked the streets in towns. Indefinite wonders touched the man's feet, his crumpled knees, and his crooked hands that were spread on his lap.

Then Tom said: "Froman, I reckon that's a prime good place to be now."

"Hit may be so, but I wouldn't be-nasty my feet with the dust of hit no longer. Nor any other place down there. I'm on my way back."

The old man's voice quavered over his words toward the close of this speech, and after a little while he added, his voice lifted: "Hit's a far piece back, but a man has a rather about where he'd like to be." Finally he spoke in great anger, his arm raised and his hand threatening: "I've swat my last drop of sweat in that-there country and eat my last meal's victuals. A man has a rather as to the place he likes to be."

This thought lay heavily over the fireplace, shared by all but uncomprehended by Nance, whose skin was rich with blood and life. She sat complacently rocking back and forth in her small chair.

After the long quiet which surrounded this thought the old man began to speak softly, having spent his passion: "I'm on my way back. I been in a study a long time about goen back but seems like I couldn't make hit to go. Work was terrible pressen. But now I'm on my way back where I was borned and my mammy and pappy before me. Many is the day I'd study about that-there and many is the night I lay awake to study about the way back over Coster Ridge, on past Bear Mountain, past Hog Run, past Little Pine Tree, up and on past Louse Run, up, then on over Long Ridge and up into Laurel, into Grady Creek and on up the branch, past the Flat Rock, past the sawmill, past the grove of he-balsams, and then the smoke a-comen outen the chimney and the door open and old Nomie's pup a-comen down the road to meet me. I'd climb the whole way whilst I was a-layen there, in my own mind I would, and I'd see the ivy as plain as you'd see your hand afore your face, and the coves and the he-balsams. In my own mind I'd go back, a step at a time, Coster, Bear Mountain and the Bee Gum, Little Pine Tree, Louse Run, Grady, and I'd see the rocks in the way to go, and a log stretched out in my way maybe. I wouldn't make hit too easy to go. Past Bear Mountain, past Hog Run and the cove, scratchen my way through ivy brush. Then I'd come to myself and there I'd be, a month's travel from as much as a sight of the Flat Rock, and I'd groan and shake and turn over again.

Nance laid a little stick on the fire, with a glance at Tom, he allowing it without protest. Then she sat back in her stiff chair with a quick movement, her bare feet light on the boards. The old man was talking again.

"Where my mammy was borned before me and her mammy and daddy before again. And no water in all Froman or Tateville but dead pump waters, no freestone like you'd want. How could a man expect to live? Many's the night I've said, could I be on the shady side of the Flat Rock, up past the sawmill, up past the grove of he-balsams, where the spring branch runs out over the horseshoe rock, and could I get me one drink of that-there cold crystal water I'd ask ne'er thing more of God Almighty in life."

"I know that-there very spring branch," Newt now said. He was eager to enter the drama of the world, and his time now had come. "I know that-there very place. You come to a rock set on end and a hemlock bush set off to the right, she-balsams all off to the left like."

"Mankind, that's just how hit's set. I believe you been right there!"

"A mountain goes straight up afore you as you stand, say this-here is the spring, and the water comes out and runs off over a horseshoe rock."

"Mankind, that's just how hit's set. I do believe you know that-there very place. You say hit's there just the same?"

"I got me a drink at that-there very spring branch Tuesday 'twas a week ago."

"You drank them waters!" And then he said after a period of wonder: "To think you been to that very spring branch! You been there!"

"We can burn another stick," Tom said, as if in honor of the strange event, and Nance mended the fire again. Outside Newt heard dogs howling far up the slope and some small beast cried.

"To think you been there! You are a-setten right now in hearen of my voice and yet a Tuesday 'twas a week ago you was in the spot I call home. Hit's hard to study over. You come down the mountain fast. That country is powerful hard goen."

"Yes, I come right fast."

"I couldn't make hit back in twice the time and more. Hard goen it was. What made you travel so hard, young man?"

"I'm a-maken hit toward the settlements."

"And what you think to find in the settlements, God knows! What you think to see, young man?"

"Learnen. I look to find learnen in the settlements."

In the pause that followed the old man gazed at the hearth as if he were looking into time, into all qualities, and he fell momentarily asleep under the impact of his gaze. But presently he looked at Newt and said: "And to think you tasted them waters Tuesday 'twas a week ago!"

"You come to a rock set on end, and here's the hemlock off to the right like, and here to the left goes the gorge."

The old man was asleep, his eyes falling away before the fire. But he waked suddenly and said with kindling eyes, his hand uplifted: "You come from there at a master pace, young man, come from the place I hope to see if God Almighty sees fitten to bless me afore I lay me down and die. You walked, I reckon, right over the spot I pined to see a many is the year, God knows, and it was nothing to you, but take care. The places you knowed when you was a little shirttail boy won't go outen your head or outen your recollections."

Then he said, another outbreak after a long pause, his hand again uplifted: "I reckon you relish learnen, young man, and take a delight in hit, and set a heap of store by the settlements. But the places you knowed when you was a little tad, they won't go outen your remembrance. Your insides is made that way, and made outen what you did when you was a shirttail boy, and you'll find it's so. Your dreams of a night and all you pine to see will go back. You won't get shed so easy of hit. You won't get shed."

Newt looked into the fire and a terror grew into his thought. He saw minutely the moss on the well curb and the shapes in which it grew, and saw the three stones that lay beside the well, that lifted his feet out of the mud. The sound made by the bucket in the well as it rocked from wall to wall, as it finally struck the water, rolled acutely backward into his inner hearing. He saw the rope twine over the beam as he turned the wooden handle, drawing the full bucket to the top. Three long steps then to the door of the house, the feel of the filled bucket drawing at his arm. Up the loft ladder to his room, his hands drawing up his body, the simple act of climbing, of emerging from some lower place to a higher, and he was buried in the act, submerged in a deep sense of it.

"You may go far and see a heap in life," the old stranger said, slowly, defiantly prophetic, "you may go far, but mark me as I say it, the places you knowed when you was a little tad will be the strongest in your remembrance. It's true, whoever you are and whatever land you come from. Your whole insides is made outen what you done first."

Newt saw in terror what he saw as he gazed into the sinking embers. His mother calling him from the house door, calling him to come to his dinner, her hand uplifted to the door frame. His sister, a little girl, dragging his chair in place and pushing his cup up against the plate. His tears for them dimmed the fire to a vague, red, quivering glow. The floating images in the dark of the well water, the bright light of the sky in the middle as a picture in a frame, and his own head looking into the heart of the picture—these were between him and the fire, moving more inwardly and dragging himself with them as they went. He was bereft, divided, emptied of his every wish, and he gazed at the fire, scarcely seeing it.

There was moving in the room, figures making a dim passage of shadows behind him. Presently he knew that the old man had gone to his sleeping place and that Nance was spreading quilts on the floor to the side of the fireplace. Her strong body was pleasant to sense as she flung out the covers and pulled them into line, and a delight in the strange room, the strange bed, welled over him. His breath was then set to a fluted rhythm as he drew suddenly inward a rich flood of air, a rhythm flowing deeply until it touched the core of his desire for the settlements, laid an amorous pulse on his determination to go there. Learning was the word he cherished and kept identified with his quickened breath. He remembered that the lights of Merryman and the settlements would be brightly dusted over the low valley when he reached Coster.

By the end of the week he would, his eager breath told him, be looking down on the farther valleys.

The Earth Poet
from God's Oddling
Jesse Stuart

WE lived by signs or what people now would call superstitions. When I was old enough to learn anything, I learned to respect the peewees. My father and mother loved those birds. And, in the little house where I lived until I was nine, a pair came each spring. My father used to say, "Must be time to plow the garden, our peewees are back." Nothing, no sign or indication, escaped my father. I recall he always told me to expect rain when the leaves spiraled up toward the sky, and so whenever I see oak leaves twisting up from the strong, sturdy boughs, turning over and showing their soapy bellies to the wind and hot sun, I know that a storm is coming and I remember my father.

Nothing ever escaped my father for he was an earth poet who loved the land and everything on it. He liked to watch things grow. From the time I was big enough for him to lead me by the hand, I went with him over the farm. If I couldn't walk all the way in those early days, he'd carry me on his back. I learned to love many of the things he loved.

I went with my father to so many fields over the years and listened to him talk so often about their beauty that I know now that he had wonderful thoughts which should have been written down. Thoughts came to him faster than a hummingbird flits from one blossom to another.

Sometime in the dim past of my boyhood, my father unloaded me from his back under some white-oak trees just beginning to leaf. "Look at this hill, son," he said, gesturing broadly with a sweep of his hand. "Look up that steep hill toward the sky. See how pretty that new-ground corn is."

This was the first field I can remember my father's taking me to see. The rows of corn curved like dark-green rainbows around a high slope with a valley and its little tributaries running down through the center. The corn blades rustled in the wind, and my father said he could understand what the corn blades were saying. He told me they whispered to each other, and this was hard for me to believe. I reasoned that before anything could speak or make a sound it had to have a mouth. When my father said the corn could talk, I got down on my knees and I looked a stalk over.

"This corn hasn't got a mouth," I told my father. "How can anything talk when it doesn't have a mouth?"

He laughed like the wind in the corn and hugged me to his knees, and we went on.

On a Sunday, when my mother and sisters were at church, my father took me by the hand and led me across two valleys to a cove where once giant beech timber had stood. He was always restless on Sundays, eager to get back to the fields in which he worked all week. He had cleared a piece of this land to raise white corn, which he planned to have ground for meal to make our bread. He thought this cove was suited to white corn. He called it Johnson County corn. Someone had brought the seed from the Big Sandy River, in the county where my father was born and lived until he was sixteen. When he had cleared this cove, set fire to the giant beech tops, and left ash over the new ground, he thought this earth would produce cornfield beans too. In every other hill of corn he had planted beans. Now these beans ran up the cornstalks and weighted them with hanging pods of young, tender beans. Pictures I saw later of Jack and the Beanstalk always reminded me of this tall corn with bean vines winding around the stalks up to the tassels.

But the one thing my father had brought me to see that delighted him most was the pumpkins. I'd never seen so many pumpkins with long necks and small bodies. Pumpkins as big around as the bottom of a flour barrel were sitting in the furrows beneath the tall corn, immovable as rocks. There were pumpkins, and more pumpkins, of all colors—yellow and white, green and brown.

"Look at this, won't you," my father said. "Look what corn, what beans, what pumpkins. Corn ears so big they lean the cornstalks. Beans as thick as honey-locust beans on the honey-locust tree. And pumpkins thicker than the stumps in this new ground. I could walk all over this field on pumpkins and never step on the ground."

He looked upon the beauty of this cove he had cleared and his three crops growing here. He rarely figured a field in dollars and cents. Although he never wasted a dollar, money didn't mean everything to him. He liked to see the beauty of growing things on the land. He carried this beauty in his mind.

Once, when we were walking between cornfields on a rainy Sunday afternoon, he pointed to a redbird on its nest in a locust tree, a redbird with shiny red feathers against the dark background of a nest. It was just another bird's nest to me until he whispered, "Ever see anything as pretty as what the raindrops do to that redbird sitting on her dark nest?" From this day on, I have liked to see birds, especially redbirds, sitting on their nests in the rain. But my father was the first one to make me see the beauty.

"A blacksnake is a pretty thing," he once said to me, "so shiny and black in the spring sun after he sheds his winter skin."

He was the first man I ever heard say a snake was pretty. I never forgot his saying it. I can even remember the sumac thicket where he saw the blacksnake.

He saw more beauty in trees than any man I have ever known. He would walk through a strange forest laying his hand upon the trees, saying this oak or that pine, that beech or poplar, was a beautiful tree. Then he would single out other trees and say they should be cut. He would always give his reasons for cutting a tree: too many trees on a root stool, too thick, one damaged by fire at the butt, one leaning against another, too many on the ground, or the soil not deep enough above a ledge of rocks to support them.

Then there were the hundreds of times my father took me to the hills to see wild flowers. I thought it was silly at first. He would sit on a dead log, maybe one covered with wild moss, somewhere under the tall beech trees, listening to the wind in the canopy of leaves above, looking at a clump of violets of percoon growing beside a rotted log. He could sit there enjoying himself indefinitely. Only when the sun went down would we get up and start for home.

My father wouldn't break the Sabbath by working, except in an emergency. He would follow a cow that was overdue to calve. He would watch over ewes in the same manner. He followed them to the high cliffs and helped them deliver their lambs, saving their lives. He would do such things on Sundays, and he would fight forest fires. But he always said he could make a living working six days in the week. Yet he was restless on Sundays. He just had to walk around and look over his fields and enjoy them.

Sometimes when I went with my father to a field, we'd cross a stream, and he'd stop the horse, sit down on the bank in the shade, and watch the flow of water. He'd watch minnows in a deep hole. He wouldn't say a word, and I wouldn't either. I'd look all around, wondering what he'd seen to make him stop, but I never would ask him. When he got through looking, he'd tell me why he'd stopped. Sometimes he wouldn't. Then we'd go on to the field together, and he'd work furiously to make up for the time he had lost while he sat beside the stream and watched the clean water flowing over the sand and gravel to some far-off place beyond his little hill world.

My father didn't have to travel over the country searching for something beautiful to see. He didn't have to go away to find beauty, for he found it everywhere around him. He had eyes to find it. He had a mind to know it. He had a heart to appreciate it. He was an uneducated poet of this earth. And if anybody had told him that he was, he wouldn't have understood. He would have turned and walked away without saying anything.

In the winter, when snow was over the ground, and the stars glistened, he'd go to the barn to feed the livestock at four in the morning. I have seen him put corn in the feedboxes for the horses and mules, then go out and stand and look at the morning moon. He once told me he always kept a horse with a flaxen mane and tail because he liked to see one run in the moonlight with his mane arched high and his tail floating on the wind.

I've gone out early in the morning with him, and he's shown me Jack Frost's beautiful architecture, which lasted only until the sun came up. This used to be one of the games my father played with me on a cold morning. He showed me all the designs that I would never have found without him. Today, I cannot look at white fields of frost on early winter mornings and not think of him.

When spring returned, he was always taking me someplace to show me a new tree he had found, or a pretty red mushroom growing on a rotting stump in some deep hollow. He found so many strange and beautiful things that I tried to rival him by making discoveries, too. I looked into the out-of-way and unexpected places to find the beautiful and the unusual.

Once, in autumn, we went to the pasture field to hunt pawpaws. "Look at the golden meat and the big brown seeds like the seeds of melon or a pumpkin," he said. "Did you ever taste a banana in your life that was as good as a pawpaw? Did you ever see anything prettier than the clean sweet golden fruit of a pawpaw?" I never forgot how he described a pawpaw, and I've always liked their taste.

He took me to the first persimmon grove I ever saw. This was after frost, and the persimmons had ripened and had fallen from the trees. "The persimmon is a candy tree," he said. "It really should have been called the gumdrop tree." I was a small boy then, but ever since I've seen ripe persimmons after frost as brown gumdrops.

I didn't get the idea of dead leaves being golden ships on the sea from a storybook. And neither did my father, for he had never read a book in his life. He'd never had a book read to him either. It was in October, and we were sitting on the bank of W-Branch. We were watching the blue autumn water slide swiftly over the slate rocks. My father picked up leaves that were shaped like little ships and dropped them into the water.

"These are ships on swift water," he told me, "going to far-off lands where strangers will see them." He had a special love for autumn leaves, and he'd pick them up when we were out walking and ask me to identify them. He'd talk about how pretty each leaf was and how a leaf was prettier after it was dead than it was alive and growing.

Many people thought my father was just a one-horse farmer who never got much out of life. They saw only a little man, dressed in clean, patched overalls, with callused and brier-scratched hands. They often saw the beard along his face. And they saw him go off and just stand in a field and look at something. They thought he was moody. Well, he was that all right, but when he was standing there and people thought he was looking into space, he was looking at a flower or a mushroom or a new bug he'd discovered for the first time. And when he looked up into a tree, he wasn't searching for a hornet's nest to burn or a bird's nest to rob. He wasn't trying to find a bee tree. He was just looking closely at the beauty in a tree. And among the millions, he always found one different enough to excite him.

No one who really knew him ever felt sorry for my father. Any feeling of pity turned to envy. For my father had a world of his own, larger and richer than the vast earth that world travelers know. He found more beauty in his acres and square miles than poets who have written a half-dozen books. Only my father couldn't write down the words to express his thoughts. He had no common symbols by which to share his wealth. He was a poet who lived his life upon this earth and never left a line of poetry—except to those of us who lived with him.

Our Heritage

Jesse Stuart

We are a part of this rough land
Deep-rooted like the tree.
We've plowed this dirt with calloused hand
More than a century.

We know each cowbell's ringing here
Which tells the time of day.
We know the slopes to plant each year,
What our folks do and say.

We know the signals of each horn
And the messages they send
At set of sun or early morn
Upon a blowing wind.

When we lie down in bed at night
And hear a foxhorn blow,
We often rise, take lantern light,
Untie our hounds and go.

We like to follow hounds that chase
The fox until the morn
Then go back home with sleepy face
And on to plow the corn.

There is not one who does not love
A field and farming ground,
With sky and stars a roof above
And a companion hound!

We love this land we've always known
That holds us and our dead—
The rugged slopes with scattered stone
That grow our daily bread.

We love the lyric barking hound
And a piping horn that trills.
We love our high upheavaled ground,
Our heritage of hills.

Heritage

James Still

I shall not leave these prisoning hills
Though they topple their barren heads to level earth
And the forests slide uprooted out of the sky.
Though the waters of Troublesome, of Trace Fork,
Of Sand Lick rise in a single body to glean the valleys,
To drown lush pennyroyal, to unravel rail fences;
Though the sun-ball breaks the ridges into dust
And burns its strength into the blistered rock
I cannot leave. I cannot go away.

Being of these hills, being one with the fox
Stealing into the shadows, one with the new-born foal,
The lumbering ox drawing green beech logs to mill,
One with the destined feet of man climbing and
    descending,
And one with death rising to bloom again, I cannot go.
Being of these hills I cannot pass beyond.

Her First Calf

Wendell Berry

Her fate seizes her and brings her
down. She's heavy with it. It
wrings her. The great weight
is heaved out of her. It eases.
She moves into what she has become,
sure in her fate now
as a fish free in the current.
She turns to the calf who has broken
out of the womb's water and its veil.
He breathes. She licks his wet hair.
He gathers his legs under him
and rises. He stands, and his legs
wobble. After the months
of his pursuit of her, now
they meet face to face.
From the beginnings of the world
his arrival and her welcome
have been prepared. They have always
known each other.

Caribou

Robert Penn Warren

Far, far southward, the forest is white, not merely
As snow of no blemish, but whiter than ice yet sharing
The mystic and blue-tinged, tangential moonlight,
Which in unshadowed vastness breathes northward.
Such great space must once
Have been a lake, now, long ages, ice-solid.

Shadows shift from the whiteness of forest, small
As they move on the verge of moon-shaven distance. They
grow clear,
As binoculars find the hairline adjustment.
They seem to drift from the purity of forest.
Single, snow-dusted above, each shadow appears, each
Slowly detached from the white anonymity
Of forest, each hulk
Lurching, each lifted leg leaving a blackness as though
Of a broken snowshoe partly withdrawn. We know
That the beast's foot spreads like a snowshoe to support
That weight, that bench-kneed awkwardness.

The heads heave and sway. It must be with spittle
That jaws are ice-bearded. The shoulders
Lumber on forward, as though only the bones could,
inwardly,
Guess destination. The antlers,
Blunted and awkward, are carved by some primitive
craftsman.

We do not know on what errand they are bent, to
What mission committed. It is a world that
They live in, and it is their life.
They move through the world and breathe destiny.
Their destiny is as bright as crystal, as pure
As a dream of zero. Their destiny
Must resemble happiness even though
They do not know that name.

I lay the binoculars on the lap of the biologist. He
Studies distance. The co-pilot studies a map. He glances at
A compass. At mysterious dials. I drink coffee. Courteously,
The binoculars come back to me.

I have lost the spot. I find only blankness.

But
They must have been going somewhere.

from

The Memory of Old Jack

Wendell Berry

SINCE before sunup Old Jack has been standing at the edge of the hotel porch, gazing out into the empty street of the town of Port William, and now the sun has risen and covered him from head to foot with light. But not yet with warmth, and in spite of his heavy sheepskin coat he has grown cold. He pays that no mind. When he came out and stopped there at the top of the steps, mindful of the way the weight of his body is taking him, he propped it carefully with his cane and, in the way that has lately grown upon him, left it.

From the barn whose vaned cupola was visible over the house roof against the pale sky, Mat Feltner was calling his cows. Old Jack listened with an eagerness that carried him away from himself; for all his consciousness of where he was, he might have been asleep and dreaming. Mat waited, and called again. And then from the quietening of Mat's voice, Old Jack knew that the cows had come near and that Mat could see them moving up deliberative and shadowy out of the mists and the thinning darkness. And then he heard the barn doors slide open.

Except for the crowing now and then of roosters, the town and its outskirts were quiet. Old Jack's mind was with Mat there in the barn, stirring about the lives of animals. He knew the solitude that Mat had entered at the beginning of every workday since his son was killed in the war. He knew the stiffness and pain that the tobacco cutting had placed in Mat's back and shoulders and hands. He was aware of the deep somnolence of the hayricks in the loft of the barn.

Alert, absent in what he knew, the old man stood on the porch in the chill whitening of the dawn, empty of himself as a public statue, while all in him that had kept most alive lived there in the waking barn with Mat. And he has continued to stand there while the cries of roosters have flared and flared again across the ridges, and the daylight and then the sunlight have come. He has heard the waking of other farms, the summoning of stock from the pastures, the occasional bawling of a cow. He has heard the tractors start, the wagons lumbering to the fields.

Though tractors draw them now, not horses and mules, there is something in the sound of the wagons going out that is the same as always. Now there is the alien commotion of iron and fire, but within it or under it there is the old rattling and pounding of the empty wagon beds against the bolsters, hurrying out over the rough farm roads in the cool of the morning. As he listened there passed and passed again across the gaze of his memory a team of good mare mules that he bought as three-year-olds from Graham Foresee in the September of 1888.

They were a team of black, mealy-nosed mare mules with plenty of size and depth of body, with a lot of lift in their motion, matched well every way. Beck and Kate. As though the reins are in his hands, and he stands again on the rattling wagon, they are carrying him to the field. The sun is just coming up. It is the fall of the year. The mules are in good flesh, the hair glossy on them, and they are fresh from the night. They step together in the harness with an eager lightness that for a moment shortens his breath.

They were the first team of their quality that he ever owned. They were, maybe, an extravagance. He bought them because he needed a team, no question about that. But he bought as carefully as he did, and paid the price he paid, in a kind of celebration of himself. He had owned his place then—or owned the debt his father had left on it—for three years. And though he had not yet cleared the farm of debt, he was clearing it. He was going to clear it. There was no longer any doubt in him about his ability to do that. It had become plain to him that he was equal to what would be required of him, and to what he would require of himself.

And so he bought the mules. He hunted until he found a pair that he could look at and use with the satisfaction of fulfilled judgment, and he paid what was necessary. He went on horseback to get them one Saturday evening after work, and led them home in the dark of the night. He missed a dance to go get them, and when something reminded him of it two or three days later, he added that to the price.

The next day he could not stay away from the barn. He led the team out after breakfast and groomed them and stood them together in the barn lot. On his own ground they still looked well to him. They suited him.

In the afternoon he brought them out again and hitched them in the driveway of the barn and busied himself repairing and adjusting a set of harness for them. Though he is at the end now, looking back at the beginning, the pleasure of that work and what it anticipated comes to him again and fills his mind.

He is sitting in the doorway of the harness room, the wide front entrance of the barn standing open at his left so that he can look out across the barn lot at the back of the old house standing gray among its trees. His knife, a punch, and several thongs of rawhide lie on the bench beside him. A breeze draws through the driveway. Used as he is to the expansive labor of the fields, he is enjoying the smallness and neatness of this task.

He hears a horse's shod hoof strike rock, and looks up to see Ben Feltner coming around the house on a gray mare; Mat, Ben's five-year-old son, is coming along behind him on a pony. Ben is married to Nancy, the only one of Jack's sisters who was still at home when he was born, and who in the years after their mother died gave him most of his upbringing. It was Nancy who encouraged Jack to buy their home place, and Ben who went on his note at the bank. A large, gentle man with the beard and eyes of a patriarch though he is not yet fifty, Ben Feltner is a widely respected farmer and citizen. He has a provident, retentive mind, the exacting judgment of a stockman, a brief, dry wit.

If Nancy was Jack's mother after his real mother died when he was five, it could be said that both after and for a good many years before the death of his real father when Jack was eighteen, Ben stood before him as a father. That was never a declared relationship. Jack was too old and too proud by the time of his father's death to accept openly a paternal authority that he had not been born under, and Ben was not the sort to give advice that had not been asked for. But Ben was the man Jack watched and listened to and checked his judgment against. There were times when Jack would outline a problem, as if hypothetically, and Ben would say carefully what he thought "a fellow" ought to do in such a circumstance.

Since he signed Jack's note for the purchase of the farm, Ben had said simply nothing at all about it. The visits he had made to Jack's place have been casual, to the point of whatever business brought him, never taking him farther than the barn. But Jack has known that he has been watched, and he has had the feeling during the last several months that he was being watched with approval. All this is characteristic of Ben, who understands the enthusiasms that pertain to beginnings, and who has therefore, in his offhand way, deferred judgment for nearly three years.

For a while they pass the time of day there in front of the barn. Jack leads out the new team of mules, and they look at them and talk about them. But Ben does not get off his horse. He has come at last, Jack realizes, to see for himself. He was getting ready to go look up his stock, Jack says. Do they want to come along? He saddles his horse and they ride together, the two men followed by the boy on the pony, out the ridge behind the barn. Letting the horses loaf along through the bright, hot afternoon, they ride over all the fields, examining the condition of the ground, the crops, the pasture, the stock, the fences and buildings. Though Jack speaks of what he has done and is doing and what he hopes to do, Ben says little. Occasionally he asks a question or speaks to his mare or points something out to Mat. At times they ride along in silence. But Jack is aware that within the shadow of his hat brim Ben's eyes are seeing and considering everything.

They stop to let Mat have a swim in a little pool, walled up in Jack's grandfather's time to catch the outflow of a spring. Jack and Ben hitch the horses and come and sit on the broad, moss-edged capstones of the wall in the shade of a huge sycamore. There comes upon them a deep pleasure in the leisurely afternoon. After Mat has dried himself in the sun and dressed and come to sit between them on the wall, they stay on, watching the little fish that live in the pool and the dragonflies that hover over it. Outside the shade of the old tree the afternoon burns bright on the slopes of the pasture.

As the day cools toward sundown they ride back to the barn. Jack dismounts at the door and speaks a few jocular parting words to Mat. And then he turns to Ben, whose eyes—pleased, and in their distant way perhaps amused—are looking at him now. "Jack, my boy, you're doing all right." He touches the mare then and turns her, Mat following, and starts home. Jack watches them out of sight.

Though he stands leaning on his cane on the porch of the hotel in Port William, looking out into the first cool morning of September, 1952, he is not there. He is four miles and sixty-four years away, in the time when he had music in him and he was light. From the height of that time his mind comes down to him, a bird to the head of a statue, and another day of his old age lights the street. The chill has gone deep in him now. He will go down to Jasper Lathrop's store, where, though it is too early in the season yet to expect a fire, some of yesterday's warmth will have been held overnight. Smiting the edge of the porch sharply with his cane as if to set hard reality on the alert, taking careful sight on the stone steps, he lets himself heavily down.

Uncle Orphy

Gail Godwin

EVERY few weeks, my widowed grandmother would sigh wistfully and say to my mother and me, "I feel like going out to see Uncle."

"Uncle" was her older brother, Orpha Rogers. She'd had a younger brother, Furman, but he was killed by a train when he was twenty-five. I called Uncle "Uncle Orphy." My mother, who liked to concoct naughty names for those close to her, called him "Uncle Orful," not to his face, of course.

"Out," where Uncle Orphy lived, was about as far as you could get from Asheville without being somewhere else altogether—or so it seemed then. Actually it was only about a thirty-minute drive. During this drive, my grandmother would elaborate on the fallen fortunes of herself and her sister Ida and her brother Orphy due to the fact that their widowed father, Frank Rogers, had married again and had a second set of children, to whom he left everything in his will. My grandmother called these children "the steps." In the mid-1800s the Rogerses had been tobacco planters and owned a great deal of land, but now even the family homestead had been sold off by Frank's grasping widow and been turned into a horrible, sprawling, tacky development. Ida had married and divorced, done fancy needlework for the Vanderbilts in Biltmore for a while, then taken her youngest daughter and gone to live in Florida; Edna, my grandmother, had married Thomas Krahenbuhl, a second-generation Swiss whose job as general foreman on the Southern Railway took her out of the mountains for much of their married life; Orpha was the only one who had stuck at home in Buncombe County, where Rogerses had always lived as far back as we could trace, which was to Orpha and Edna's great-grandfather Robert Rogers, who was born at the end of the eighteenth century.

After a prolonged drive, the mountain roads narrowing from pavement to gravel to dirt, the craggy pastures on either side tilting so alarmingly skyward that I couldn't understand how the poor cows kept their balance while they ate, there we would be at the bottom of Uncle's steps.

There were so many steps that you couldn't even see the log house at the top, where behind the screen door Aunt Fanny's long, skull-thin face would already have materialized at the first sound of our car. Since I was the only one who didn't have to stop on all those stairs for breath, I was always the first to see this rather spectral welcome floating at us from behind the screen door.

Inside was cool and somewhat dark; in winter, there would be a fire in the woodstove. There was a framed picture I liked over the sofa, some old magazine illustration: I think it was of a pretty young woman in a thin white dress climbing down (or up) a steep cliff in the moonlight, but maybe it wasn't. The house smelled of roasting meats and stewed fruits and beans and cornbread if we were there for a meal, and of freshly baked cake and biscuits if we could only stay for tea. Fanny made fresh biscuits three times a day, my grandmother said, because Orpha never could stand eating a cold biscuit. I knew I must "sit still" for some family gossip and answer a few questions about myself; then, until summoned to Fanny's groaning table, I would be released to the outdoors where I could climb the chinaberry tree with branches low enough for me, or go and sit in the outhouse, which fascinated me with its two holes in the long wooden seat and its stack of magazines and the dank, woodsy smell overpowered by the strong odor of Pine-Sol.

Uncle sat in his chair, waiting for us. He had a fleshless face like his wife and a long, arched, bony nose exactly like my grandmother's. One of his blue eyes had no pupil ("A nail flew up and put it out," he told me matter-of-factly), and I tried not to stare at its blank pale center. In earlier years, he always stood up and allowed his sister and niece to hug and kiss him, then bent down and, with a long-suffering, good-humored, "*Ohhhh,* me," hugged his grandniece. He smelled at various times of fertilizer, leather, wet animal pelts, fresh milk, starch, and Octagon soap. In later years he remained seated, his knobbly hand resting patriarchally on top of his hickory cane, and, uttering the same "*Ohhhh,* me," allowed us each in turn to bend down and plant kisses in his sparse white hair.

He referred to himself always as O.M. Rogers and signed his letters to us that way: "Hope I see you again sometime. Buy you a remembrance with this little green paper. your uncle, OMR."

He wrote this to me inside a "Hello There!" greeting card when he was ninety-three and I was in my thirties. The date was March 23, 1975; he would live three more years. It wasn't my birthday; perhaps I had been to see him on a recent visit to Asheville and he had enjoyed me. I used to make him laugh, not always intentionally. Once I entered his house and he took one look at me, said "*Ohhhh,* me," and began to chuckle til he held his sides. It was my new haircut, which, I realize in retrospect, must have made me resemble a frizzled mushroom. In one of my "serious" phases, he leaned forward in his chair and inquired anxiously, "Do you ever let *little things* bother you?" Surprised and rather pleased by what I thought for him was a personal question, I confided at once, "I'm afraid I do, Uncle Orphy."

"Then . . . ," he paused for effect, "don't ever sleep in the same room with a mosquito." He doubled over in soundless laughter.

On one of my last visits to him—now I, too, had to pause and catch my breath halfway up those Himalayan steps—I got up the nerve to ask him what the "M" in his name stood for. Nobody knew or would tell me.

"Montraville," he said, shaking his head. "Isn't that awful? I never tell people. I think it was something my mother found in a book."

He eschewed alcohol and tobacco. "After Mother and Fanny died," my mother writes in her unfinished autobiography, "I kept up my visits to Uncle and took him my Christmas tree cookies (which I'm sure he would not have touched if he had known the icing was made with rum or brandy); at Easter I took him flowers and he always said I shouldn't have spent my money on him."

But in a lengthy newspaper tribute written about him on his ninety-sixth birthday ("A Testimony to Good Living"), he contradicts his daughter Helen, who has just told *Asheville Citizen* columnist Bob Terrell that her daddy never smoked or drank.

"Yes, I did. I smoked once. I rolled a cigar out of tobacco leaf and smoked it. There was a wagon sitting there and first thing I knew, that wagon started going round and round. I dove under it and when I sobered up I come out. I drank one time, too. When beer come out, I got two bottles and put 'em in the icebox. When they got cold, I opened one up, took two sups, and thought I'd never tasted anything that bad. I poured the rest of it out and gave the other bottle away."

There were other stories in the tribute, stories I vaguely remembered, or had forgotten parts of, from his own telling. Bob Terrell had been a sharp listener, and I was grateful to him for keeping the language the way my great-uncle would have spoken it; Terrell also caught the deadpan quality of my uncle's narratives, and it was like hearing Uncle Orphy speak when I was at last old enough to pay full attention.

There was his story of Asheville's Great Flood of 1916, which washed away his store at the east end of Craggy Bridge.

"That flood was something! I was sitting here on my front porch and a man came by from [Craggy Bridge]. I asked him, 'How's the river over there?' and he said, 'Pretty bad. Rogers Store just washed away.' I said, 'I better go see.' Sure enough, it was gone. People told me it just washed loose and floated away. Down the river a ways it hit a tree and turned upside down and all the goods come out of it and floated away. There was a lot of goods in that store."

A young man Orpha and Fanny had raised like a son waded into the water and got into the upside down store and managed to get the papers and deeds out of the safe. "That was a huge safe. We found it later buried in the sand down the river bottom. We poked around with a steel rod till we found it, but when I hooked a team of mules to it and tried to pull it out, they pulled the knob off and ruined it."

He loved to ride horses, and when I was a little girl, he put me astride an enormous pig and let me ride it. In the Terrell piece there was also the story about the one time he rode a motorcycle. He was so exhilarated by the experience, he zipped by his house and told Fanny to hop on. "We headed up this dirt road and it was pretty bumpy. I had to pay attention to where I was going, and when I looked back, Mother wasn't there. I turned around and went back down the road and found her. She'd bounced off, but luckily wasn't hurt."

He served as a deputy under three sheriffs. One day the sheriff called and told him two escaped prisoners were headed his way toward the bridge. One of these was one-armed and had a coat hanging over that shoulder. Orpha got to the bridge just in time to see two strange men coming from the other side, and one of them had a coat hanging off his shoulder.

"I slapped him on that side and he didn't have an arm, so I told them they were under arrest. The other one grabbed my pistol and took off, but I held onto the one-armed man and took him in. I heard later that the other one went to New York, got with another partner, and went to rob a post office. They tied up the clerk and laid my pistol on a shelf while they gathered up what they wanted. The clerk worked his way loose, got my pistol, and killed both of 'em. Took me three months to get my pistol back."

Orpha and Fanny, like true mountain people, were a hospitable couple. Anyone who showed up close to mealtime, even a stranger, was invited to stay for a meal. Their daughter Helen told my mother that during Fanny's last days in the nursing home, she hallucinated that her house was full of people and said to Helen they must hurry and get enough food prepared for all these people and make up beds for them.

At Fanny's funeral, my mother writes in the autobiography she didn't live to finish, Orpha's half-niece, daughter of one of the "steps," a beautician who always insisted she was "really more of a Rogers than the other side," grabbed his arm ahead of his own daughters and walked him up the aisle. Mother reports, "I heard him say to her what I thought at the time was 'Don't leave me,' but it wasn't that at all, I later learned. It was 'Don't *lead* me.' After the funeral, I took [the half-niece] back to the beauty shop and went on home. She called me from time to time and I would call her. Once she said she had a new bathing suit and it was prettier than any dress she had ever had. 'I want to be buried in that bathing suit,' she told me. But she wasn't."

Adios, Miss Em

Janice Holt Giles

INTO the silence of the sunny morning, into the peace of the petunia bed, bedlam suddenly broke. From the orchard there came the variously pitched yells, screams, shrieks and whoops of several children, the deep ragged howling of a dog and the ear-splitting, yowling squalls of an enraged cat.

Miss Em's reflexes were good. They caused her to yank so vigorously at the weed she was pulling that it was suddenly uprooted and she was sent reeling back into the thorny embrace of the rambler rose. "Drat!" she said vehemently. Then, plucking herself loose from the rose's prickly clutches, she marched to the orchard.

Three round-eyed little boys watched her coming. They were lined up like stair steps, their faces apprehensive. "Seth—Paul—Jimmy," she said, calling the roll down the line from the tallest to the shortest, "I've told you about teasing Augustine."

It was a ridiculous name for a cat, but she had had no choice in the matter. It had been given her by the German yard man, who when in his cups had a sentimental fondness for singing "Ach, du lieber Augustin." She had no great love for the animal, but she was afraid it would come to harm if she turned it out.

"Yes ma'am, Miss Em, but we weren't teasing him. Ring was chasing him and we were trying to make him stop," the oldest boy explained.

Miss Em reflected that their efforts would have been confusing to a dog of more intelligence than Ring. With him, she was certain they had been an encouragement. "Can't you keep your dog tied up?"

Reproachfully the three stared at her. "He likes to play with us," the smallest boy offered.

Of course he did. Miss Em sighed. When you took in little boys you invariably took in a dog, though nothing had been said about a dog when she had rented the orchard to the pipeliner and his family.

It had been a mistake, she thought, to let him put his trailer in the orchard. But money was so short, and the orchard was so shady and quiet, and people had to live somewhere. Her conscience would have disturbed her if she had refused the man.

"We won't bother a thing," he had promised, looking longingly at the big, tree-shaded space. "It's so far from the house you'll never know we're there. It would be such a fine place for the boys."

"All right," she had agreed reluctantly. It *was* a fine place for boys and the Chamber of Commerce said the townspeople must all be hospitable to the pipeline crew. After all, they were bringing thousands of dollars' worth of business to the town, as well as a natural-gas line. "But it's just for the summer," she reminded him. "Three months is all we want, ma'am. We'll be moving on then." They had arrived only a week ago. She remembered how all three of the boys lined up behind the fence the day they had moved in, solemn, curious and watchful as she trimmed the grass edges of the walk. Forty years of teaching school had given her a considerable knowledge of children. She worked on quietly, ignoring them, giving them time to absorb her and the white house and the big lawn. Suddenly, solemnly and in order they proffered their names.

"I'm Seth."

"I'm Paul."

"I'm Jimmy."

"How do you do?" she had said, turning to look at them. "I'm Miss Em."

"I'm seven."

"I'm six."

Five pudgy brown fingers went up from Jimmy. "I'm five."

They waited, two pairs of blue eyes, one of brown, fixed on her expectantly. Miss Em cleared her throat.

Jimmy, whose thumb was hovering near his mouth, asked, "How old are you?"

Paul, the middle one, nudged him and hissed, "Sh-h-h! You not s'posed to ask ladies how old they are."

Jimmy's eyes had widened. "Why?"

"They don't like to tell."

The big brown eyes had come round to rest fearfully on her, conscious of having sinned.

She had relieved him by sensibly explaining to them that they could play in the orchard but not in the yard. They must not tease the cat. They must not bother the garden tools in the shed. They could hang a swing from one of the apple trees but not the peach. They could sail their boats in the little pond at the foot of the orchard, but they must not wade in it because it grew deep at one end. Then she had given them cookies, and after thanking her gravely and meticulously they had marched off home.

Their mother was a harried, tense young woman—harried and tense not only from the constant coping with their boundless energy but from the necessity of moving every few months. She had sighed her dislike of it to Miss Em the first day. "It's no way for children to live, and I know it. But Harry's always been a pipeliner and I guess he always will be. I just have to make the best of it."

Miss Em supposed she did try, and it was not really her fault that in one week the boys had broken a limb from an apple tree, smashed the window of the tool shed, torn three palings from the fence and reduced Augustine to a quivering mass of nerves. Three times in three days she had rescued him. The boys must learn there were consequences.

She faced the stair steps. Seth and Paul were very blond and their eyes brilliantly blue. Jimmy had brown eyes and a wide smile that made dimples under his ears. His thumb sought his mouth in his uncertainty now, and his brown eyes were almost liquid with anxiety.

She must seem an ogre to him, she thought, an old-maid ogre who measured out nothing but scolding words. She knew their mother must have threatened them with, "If you don't be good Miss Em will make us move."

She wanted to reassure him; she could never bear to see a child frightened. But the schoolroom had taught her that discipline, to be effective, must be stern. Smiles were for rewards. She kept her face sober. "You'll have to get Augustine down from that tree," she said.

Three pairs of eyes turned to look at the tree. The lowest limb was far from the ground. Three pairs of eyes, full of misgiving, turned then to look at her. "Gosh, Miss Em," said Seth, "it's too big a tree to climb."

Paul, who had freckles and big ears, eyed the tree measuringly. "I can shinny up it if you'll give me a boost."

She shook her head. "You're too heavy for me to lift."

Jimmy's eyes rested on her swimmingly. "Am I too heavy?"

He's afraid to climb, she thought, but he will, if necessary. "You're too heavy, too. You'll have to think."

"Daddy can get him down when he comes home tonight."

"No, you must get him down yourselves. It's only fair. Your dog chased him up the tree. I expect you to bring him home by lunchtime." She walked away, leaving them with their problem. Was it too big? she wondered.

It was very quiet in the orchard for perhaps fifteen minutes; then there was a great banging and clattering, a few shouted orders, excitement in uplifted voices, a yell or two, a squeak of some kind, then quiet again. After a few moments it started all over, and it continued, off and on, for perhaps an hour. Miss Em went on with her weeding. They're building a ladder, she told herself, and a very sensible thing it was of them to do, too. Give a child a task and leave him alone with it. It had been a maxim of hers.

She dug out dandelions, uprooted crabgrass, stung her hands on thistle and dock, conscious of the noises in the orchard but not at all apprehensive about them. The sun was almost directly overhead when she heard them coming. She could not have missed hearing, for they were chattering loudly in their excitement. They rounded the corner and broke into a run.

"Hey, Miss Em! We got him!"

She straightened to look. They were grimy, their shirttails were out, there was a big rent in Seth's pants, but they did indeed have Augustine. Jimmy was carrying him, cradling him gently as if he were a baby. Proudly he handed him over.

"Fine," she said calmly, stroking the cat. "How did you manage?"

"Oh, we built a ladder. Come see, Miss Em. We built a dandy tree ladder."

She put the cat in the house and followed the boys to the orchard. She stared in amazed dismay. Marching rakishly up the trunk of the tree, no two slanted alike, were four palings from the fence. The fence, she saw, was now gap-toothed on both sides of the gate. She might as well, she thought bitterly, take the gate down, too. Nothing could be more unnecessary. Dear Lord, she thought, just let me get through this summer! Just give me patience for the next three months!

The boys were looking at her expectantly, waiting for her praise. "Isn't it a dandy ladder, Miss Em? Look, you can go up in a zip! Watch me, Miss Em!" Paul's legs twinkled up the slats and he straddled the lowest limb.

"Move over. I'm coming up too!" Seth scrambled up the slats and joined him. "It's easy, Miss Em. You could do it, too."

"I doubt it," she said dryly. Jimmy stood, his thumb in his mouth, watching. "Did you get Augustine down for me, Jimmy?

The thumb popped out. "Didn't any of us. He jumped down by hisself when Seth went up after him. But I caught him when he tried to run away."

"That was very thoughtful of you." She measured him a wan smile and was rewarded with an ear-dimpling grin. Well, she was hoist with her own petard. And they *had* used initiative, even if at the expense of her fence. She must be fair. "It's a fine ladder, boys," she called up the tree. "Come down now and I'll give you some lemonade and cookies."

They drank a gallon of lemonade and ate a whole batch of cookies, then wandered aimlessly over the house. In a schoolroom Miss Em knew what to do with children. In her own home she was at a loss. She let them wander. They ended up in the living room, gazing around curiously. "You've got a guitar," Seth pointed out.

"Yes."

"Do you know how to play it?"

It was her one musical accomplishment, though it had been years since she had touched the instrument. She picked it up. As a girl she had played, and the feel of the instrument in her hands now brought back memories of summer picnics on the river; of boys and girls long since grown, married, many of them dead; of the one man she might herself have married, given a few more moonlit nights—but there had been a death in his family and he had had to go away. She thought of the skating in the winter and hay rides and the taffy pulls. The guitar had accompanied them all. "Play something for us," Jimmy urged.

Self-consciously, she tried to think of a song and came up with a ballad, a very slow and sad one. She sang all its verses, gathering courage as she went along, while the boys stood in front of her, watching her hands, listening respectfully. "Gee," they said when she had finished, "that was pretty, Miss Em."

"We know a song," Seth volunteered.

"Do you? If you'll sing it, I'll try to accompany you."

"It's 'The Chisholm Trail.' "

She had never heard of it. "Start singing and I'll pick it up."

They lined up and cleared their throats. A little shyly they looked at one another, then Paul nudged Seth. "You start off."

Seth stared at his feet a moment, then lifted his head and began singing. The other boys chimed in. "Come along, boys, and I'll tell you my tale; I'll tell you my troubles on the old Chisholm Trail. Come a ki-yi-yippee, yippee-ay, come a ki-yi-yippee, yippee-ay!"

My goodness, Miss Em thought, a cowboy song! Valiantly she struggled to find the key and keep the rhythm. It was difficult, because as verse followed verse and the boys gained confidence they increased the speed of the song, until at the end they were racing madly and her fingers were having to fly.

"Well," she said, feeling out of breath, "that was fine, wasn't it?"

In a way it had been fine. Their voices were small, but sweet and very true, and they had swung along very gallantly. She put the guitar away. "I think you'd better run along now. Your mother probably has your lunch ready."

Without question they accepted the suggestion, flung themselves out of the house, banging the screen door behind them, calling back over their shoulders, "*Adios*, Miss Em. *Adios.* We'll come to see you again sometime."

Adios? Then she remembered they were from Texas.

She hadn't expected them back so soon, however. At what seemed the crack of dawn the next morning she was roused by a loud knocking at her back door. Who in the world? she wondered, reaching for a robe and trying to wedge her feet into mismatched slippers. Only half awake, she fumbled toward the door. The knocking was very insistent. "I'm coming! I'm coming!" she shouted impatiently.

In sleepy disenchantment she eyed them as they stood lined up on her steps. "What are you boys doing here at this time of day?"

"We aren't boys, ma'am," Seth told her sternly. "We're the men from the zoo. We've come to build a cage for your tiger. I'm Mr. White."

"I'm Mr. Brown."

Jimmy giggled. "I'm Mr. Black."

"We heard your tiger is giving you a lot of trouble and we've come to fix a cage for him."

"For heaven's sake, Seth," she began.

"Miss Em, a tiger is a very dangerous animal," he interrupted her eagerly. "And they shouldn't be allowed to run loose. Besides," he warned her, "it's against the law."

She saw that they had dragged along a wooden orange crate. "Oh, all right," she said. It was probably the quickest way to be rid of them.

"Where do you want to build it?"

"Here on the back porch, where you can watch him." Seth gave her a winsome smile. "You'll have to feed him and it'll be handy."

They dragged in the crate and she wondered what more they could do to it. It looked very substantial as it was. Then she saw they had other tools besides a hammer and some nails. Seth had a can opener and a screwdriver. Jimmy had a burned-out radio tube and a discarded wire sieve. They clustered around the crate, examining it in detail. "We'd better fix the spurlix first," Seth said, nodding his head wisely. "The konker has come unkonked."

Spurlix? Konker? Miss Em sat on a stool, curious now. They went to work, banging, measuring, attaching things, bending, listening, frowning, their hands flying about; "Hand me the bixter," Seth said to Jimmy, "Not the big bixter, the little one."

"We didn't bring the little bixter. Here's the skootak."

Jimmy handed him the wire sieve. There was a silence and then Seth said, "The squamlet won't do, either. What about the sticklebit?"

Paul handed over the screwdriver. Seth shook his head. "The sticklebit is too little. Mr. Black, you'll just have to go back and get the little bixter."

Jimmy hustled out the door, giving her a grin as he passed. He came back with an old toothpaste tube, thrust it at Seth. "Here, Mr. White."

Seth took it, dropped it in the tomato can, tied one end of the electric cord around the can and the other around the can opener, poked the can opener through the wire sieve and attached the whole to a crack in the wooden crate. He buzzed like a saw for a moment, then Paul began buzzing and finally Jimmy started buzzing, too. They buzzed at different speeds and in different keys for several minutes; then Seth nodded his head. "It's okay, men. Miss Em, I think your tiger will be perfectly comfortable in this nice cage."

They gathered up the hammer and nails and filed past her to the door. Dazedly, she watched them. As they reached the door, Jimmy turned around and gave her a seraphic smile. "If you have any trouble, Miss Em, just call us. Our telephone number is eleven-twenty-thirty."

She nodded, speechless.

They were halfway across the lawn before an uncontrollable impulse struck her. "Boys," she called, "just what *did* you do to the cage?"

Over the stretch of lawn, over the rosebushes, over the petunias, came Seth's clear, looping answer. "Why, Miss Em, we put in an air conditioner."

As the summer wore on she became accustomed to their visits at any hour of the day. She became accustomed to all their whimsical pretend games and learned to take her part in them easily and deftly. She was once an admiral when an expedition sailed for the North Pole. Earnestly, Seth explained that the North Pole had come loose and the President wanted them to go find it. "It won't do to have it floating loose in the ocean, Miss Em."

"Of course not," she agreed.

Feeling not the least bit silly, she stood at the helm of a tin washtub while Paul, in the crow's nest on the stepladder, called down sailing directions to her.

Once she was a policeman looking for stolen jewels, flashing a cereal-box-top badge. Handsomely, they let her shoot the robbers when they were tracked down, and, flushed and excited, she pulled the trigger on Jimmy's water pistol too soon and got them all wet.

Once she was a spaceman, a cut-out plastic vegetable bag over her head for a helmet. Once she died dramatically, hanged as a cattle rustler. That was when she had objected to riding a wooden sawhorse on the range. "You can be the cattle rustler," they had said. She had a rope burn on her neck for a week from the hanging. The boys' mother was aghast.

"Miss Em, *don't* let them bother you so much."

"Oh," she said vaguely, "they don't bother me. I send them along home when they make little nuisances of themselves."

But she didn't fool even herself. She did not know when they had ceased being three little boys who threatened the peace and quiet of her first summer of retirement and became instead three good friends. She did not know when she began to know them as persons, know that Seth was tense, nervous, sensitive and brilliant; that Paul was clever, loyal and determined; that Jimmy was docile, sweet, even-tempered. It just happened very gradually, until she found she was taking care with each, remembering his own personality, his own individuality.

Little by little she got used to them, to their casual "Hi, Miss Em" when they came, and their equally casual "*Adios,* Miss Em" when they left, to their noise and their games, until one day when their mother took them away for the day she had an odd feeling of loneliness in the big house. It was too quiet. The silence itself was very loud, and she realized that she had become so accustomed to their noise that it was like the birds in the trees, the jar flies humming their endless songs all the long, hot days, the tree frogs croaking hoarsely at night. It was strange, she thought, what one could get used to. She was used to children, of course, but not in her home. Her home had always been a cool, lofty retreat for her, her own quiet domain. Now it was the domain of the boys.

Not that they were always noisy. They came quietly sometimes, and she fed them and played the guitar for them. And they played with Augustine.

She had kept him in the house since the adventure with the dog, in the beautifully air-conditioned wooden crate. The boys all adored him, played with him, stroked him, held him, petted him, fed him. "Isn't he soft?" they said, rubbing their hands down his fur.

"Doesn't he make a funny noise inside?" holding him close to their ears.

They felt they owned him since they had rescued him from a tree and made him a cage.

So it was with a guilty feeling Miss Em had to tell them one morning that he had gone away for a little while. "Just on a little adventure," she said reassuringly. "He'll be home tonight."

Fervently, she hoped he would. He had been so restless the night before, mewing uneasily and scratching at the door, refusing his food and pacing from his box to the door. Finally she had let him out. "It's very silly of you," she told him. "You'll just get into a fight. You'd better stay home where you belong."

But he had been off like a shot, leaving her only a wave of his tail in gratitude.

He did not come home that night, however, though she called and the boys called. Nor the next day, nor the next night. They went to look for him. They looked in every tree in the orchard, in the long grass beside the pond, in the woods and meadows beyond the orchard.

"He's just gone, Miss Em," Jimmy said tearfully. "He's been kilt, I betcha."

"Oh, I don't think so," she said, trying to comfort him. "He'll come home by and by."

Each day they looked, the boys mournful and disconsolate, Miss Em increasingly anxious. He had never stayed away so long before. She grew to dread the mornings when the boys appeared, hope on their faces that she had to watch fade as she shook her head.

"Drat the animal," she said to herself. "Where can he have got to?"

It was a week to the day that she found him in the back yard, alive, but only barely. One ear was almost torn off; he was tattered and torn, bloody and clawed. Her first thought was, the boys mustn't see him like this.

She took him in the house, cleaned him up, bandaged the worst places and had him in his box on a bed of clean rags by the time they came. They were overjoyed that he had come home, hung over his box and crooned to him, but they were horrified at the sight of his condition.

"Was he in a fight, Miss Em?"

Grimly she said he must have been. The nature of tomcats was best left unexplained, she thought.

"Will he get well?"

"I hope so, but he's very sick."

They suggested remedies. "Maybe he needs a shot of penicillin."

"Maybe he needs a tetanus shot."

"Maybe if you gave him a vitamin pill?"

"We'll call the vet," she promised.

They hovered when the man came, watching his face for a clue. "He's injured internally, Miss Em," he said finally. "He's slowly bleeding to death. Shall I put him away easily?"

Her heart thumped. Death, she thought. Do they know about it?

"What does he mean, Miss Em?" It was Jimmy tugging at her skirt.

Well, it had to be faced. "He means perhaps he should put Augustine to sleep quietly, since he can't live."

"Kill him?" Seth asked quickly.

"Well, yes . . ."

Like an explosion it came from all three. "No! He can't kill him, Miss Em. He might live."

The man looked at her and she shook her head. The boys had decided.

They were tireless in their efforts to help the cat, lifting him, turning him, trying to get him to eat. They all were beside him when the end came on a hot, sultry afternoon. It was Paul who said quietly, "I think he's dead, Miss Em."

"How do you know?"

"He's stopped breathing."

Strangely enough, there were no tears now. They had agonized over his illness, hung over him, wept over him, but quite calmly they accepted his death. Even Jimmy only stroked the silky fur and said, "Poor Augustine, poor Augustine. You're dead now, Augustine."

She had expected tears and tantrums. Instead, Seth said gently, "We have to have the funeral now."

"What do you know about funerals?"

"Oh, on TV they have them. We can put him in a box and dig a grave, Miss Em."

Well, he had to be buried. She rummaged around and found a box, lined it with tissue paper, lifted Augustine into it. Gravely the boys took it outside and she showed them where to dig. "Back of the tool shed," she said. She left them then, thinking perhaps they would rather have their funeral alone.

It was Jimmy who appeared at the door. "You'd better come now. We're ready."

She followed him. They had dug a deep hole, which they had lined with grass. The box was covered with flowers. It lay beside the open hole. The three boys stood solemnly at one side. They had gone home, she saw, and put on their best clothes, washed their hands and faces, wet down their hair. Seth was officiating. When she joined them, he said, "Bow your heads. We've got to pray. You want to say the blessing, Jimmy?

Three crew-cut heads and Miss Em's own iron-gray were soberly bent while Jimmy's sweetest, most innocent voice chanted, "Come, Lord Jesus, be our guest; let this food by Thee be blessed. Amen."

Miss Em gulped. But a table grace wasn't the worst graveside prayer that could be said, she supposed.

Seth took charge again authoritatively. "Now we got to sing. All join hands."

Obediently they made a circle around the grave. Seth cleared his throat and hummed a note or two. Then he started the song, "Come along, boys, and I'll tell you my tale . . ." The others chimed in generously. "I'll tell you my troubles on the old Chisholm Trail. Come a ki-yi-yippee, yippee-ay, yippee-ay, come a ki-yi-yippee, yippee-ay."

"You're not singing, Miss Em," Jimmy accused her at the end of the first chorus. "Everybody's got to sing, don't they, Seth?"

Solemnly, Seth nodded.

Miss Em sang, "Come a ki-yi-yippee, yippee-ay."

Augustine was being gathered to the last corral, where no doubt he would join Old Paint. She might as well help herd him on his way.

For some reason they didn't want to go home that evening. She fed them and then they all sat on the wide front porch and watched the first stars come out, listened to the whippoorwills, looked at the fireflies lighting the early dark. Jimmy crawled into Miss Em's lap, put his thumb in his mouth and sleepily snuggled against her. They wanted to talk, and they talked about death and God and day and night and fairy princesses and airplanes and diesel locomotives. Then they wanted stories and Miss Em told them until her throat ached.

Jimmy was asleep when their father came for them, and he lifted the little boy gently from Miss Em's lap. It felt empty and cold where he had been.

"Come on, boys. It's nearly bedtime."

Drowsily, the other two boys clambered down from the swing where they had been flanking Miss Em, began to say good night.

"We'll be pulling out tomorrow, Miss Em," their father said. "The job's finished here."

"So soon?" she said, startled.

"The summer's over, Miss Em. I expect you'll be glad to see us go, at that. These boys have been a bother to you, I know."

Oh, no, she cried silently, one hand reaching out to touch a bristly young head. Bothered me? Not ever. Why, what would she do without them? How would the days ever be filled again?

"Good night."

They were swallowed up in the dark.

She didn't sleep that night. He had taken her by surprise. Of course, it was the first of September. He had said three months when he rented the orchard. It had been three months, but she was still unprepared for it. It had seemed no time at all. She had almost lost count of the days, so busy the summer had been, so full, so very full. She counted over the days and the memories. Yes, the three months were gone. Ruefully she remembered asking the Lord to give her patience to get through the time. She wished she could ask him now to give her just one more golden day.

She was up before the sun, made her coffee and sat and watched out the window. She wanted to see the boys once more, but she didn't know whether she should or not. She hadn't said goodbye. She had been too stunned. Perhaps it was better this way. Just let them slip out of her life. It would do no good to tell them goodbye. This summer would fade from their memories—they were so young. They would not long remember Miss Em. Seth might, and maybe Paul, but Jimmy? She remembered how soft and snuggly he had been in her lap last night. In forty years of teaching she had often comforted a hurt child, a sick child, a bewildered child; but never, not once, had one crawled into her lap and gone to sleep there, as if she had been his mother. Jimmy was too little—he would not remember her.

Unhappily, she stared out the window, and then she saw them coming, as they had so often come early in the morning, Seth leading, Paul following, Jimmy bringing up the rear. She met them at the door.

"We brought you some presents." Seth offered his.

"We made 'em." Paul offered his.

"But you're not s'posed to open 'em till we're gone." It was Jimmy offering his.

They were flat, thin little packages, wrapped in grocery paper, tied with dirty twine. Gravely she accepted them. "Thank you very much."

In a quick, smothering flurry of wiry arms, she was hugged and wetly kissed; their heels flashed over the grass and they were gone. From the orchard their voices floated back. "*Adios,* Miss Em. We'll come back and see you sometime." Oh, do, her heart wept, do! But she knew they never would.

Inside, she waited until her eyes had stopped blurring before opening their gifts. On a shirt cardboard each had drawn a picture and colored it with crayons. Seth's was a flowery wreath, with "To Miss Em from Seth" lettered in red inside. Paul's was a heart, thrust through with an arrow, also inscribed, "To Miss Em." Jimmy's was a very stark and realistic picture of a cat, stiff and dead. "Augustine," he had labeled it simply.

She heard a motor start and went to the door. The trailer was swinging around, battened down now, empty, headed home to Texas. The boys were on the back seat of the car that was pulling the trailer. Catching a glimpse of her, they waved hysterically, kept waving until they disappeared at last down the drive.

Miss Em waved, too, as long as she could see them, and just as the car turned onto the highway called, although they could not hear, "Goodbye! Goodbye!" Then fiercely, lovingly, she whispered, "*Adios* . . . Oh, *adios, amigos.*"

Wild Plums

Jesse Stuart

"THIS morning is too beautiful for one to stay in a schoolroom," thinks Principal Jason Stringer. "April has come again. The green is getting back to the hills. Men are plowing in the fields. I want to get out of the schoolroom. I want to see the tender green leaves on the water birches by the Tygart River. I want to smell the percoon blossoms. I want to see the wild plums blooming by the Tygart."

Jason Stringer fumbles the papers on the desk in his office. He checks the absentee lists of students sent from the home rooms in the Mason High School. After Jason checks the papers over again, he places them on his desk. He walks to the window. He looks at the water birches down by the Tygart River. He sees a redbird sitting on a water-birch twig. "Tea-kettle, tea-kettle, thirt, thirt, thirt," are the words he thinks it sings over and over. Soon he sees the redbird's mate fly from a Tygart bottom with a straw in her bill. She alights beside her mate. Her body is not as red as her mate's body. She sits beside him and listens to his song.

"Eustacia, we have a lot of absentees this morning," says Principal Jason Stringer. "I want you to make me out a list of all the couples that you think are playing truant together. You know more about the love affairs of these high-school students than I do. I know it's strange that there's the same number of girls absent today that there are boys. Couple them together the best you can and let me have the list."

"All right, Mr. Stringer," she says, "but don't you tell the students that I did this. I don't want them to know. They will get mad at me if they find this out."

"I'll not tell where I got my information," says Jason Stringer. "I just want to stop this playing truant. Young couples are out strolling around over these hills when they should be in school. What kind of a high school will the parents of this district think we have here? They will think we have a courting high school."

"Mr. Stringer," says Eustacia with a smile, "you remember this happened last spring. It happened spring before last. When April comes the students do their best to slip out."

"And by twos," snaps Jason Stringer. "Students that make the best grades in Mason High School, slip out when April comes to these Kentucky hills."

"When a day is as pretty as today, you can't blame them much," says Eustacia. "As I came to school this morning, I stopped by the Tygart bridge and listened to a redbird sing. I was almost late for school. The redbird was sitting there and sang until his mate flew to the top of the water-birch tree and sat beside him with a straw in her bill. I just thought it was strange how the rooster redbird did the singing while his mate built the nest."

Eustacia looks over the absentee sheets. Jason Stringer stands by the office window and looks toward the Tygart River. He can see a green streak of timber along its winding banks. The high rocky bluffs above the Tygart are covered with budding oaks. Jason can see white spots on these bluffs that look like patches of late March snow the sun hasn't melted yet. These are patches of percoon in bloom among the rock cliffs on the coves.

"Mr. Stringer," says Eustacia, "there are forty-one absent. There are twenty girls and twenty-one boys."

"Who is the odd boy, Eustacia?" Jason asks.

"Dick Martin," she says. "He never goes with a girl."

"That's right," says Jason Stringer, "but you can't tell about what he will do. He's one of the best athletes this school has ever had. He's the best track man we've got but his grades are none too good. We have a track meet with Manchester and Dick will be ineligible. Do you think he is the boy that isn't paired off with a girl?"

"I know he is," says Eustacia. "I've got a lot of confidence in Dick."

"Now you be sure to arrange these couples, Eustacia," says Principal Jason Stringer, "and leave the list in the drawer of my table. You answer all telephone calls. You take care of this office. Don't tell anybody where I am. I'm going to go out and look around. These students should know what the penalty is for playing hooky in this school. First offense it is three days' suspension. Second offense it is three weeks' suspension and—"

"Third offense," Eustacia continues, "you expel them from school—oh, we know that, Mr. Stringer."

"But the sad thing about it," Jason emphasizes, "you students know about it; yet, you continue to play truant from Mason High School every April. I think many names on that list have played truant twice and a few have played truant three times."

Jason leaves Eustacia at the desk putting this boy's name by that girl's name. He leaves her arranging the names by twos. "It will be hard on their grades," thinks Jason as he walks out of the schoolhouse. "It will be hard on me as a high-school principal when the patrons of this district find out that forty-one students out of an enrolment of 310 are out gallivanting. I'll just have to do something about it. What will the Greenwood County Superintendent of Schools and the five members of the Greenwood County School Board say to me?"

Jason bends over when he walks around the front side of the school building so that the students and the teachers can't see him from the windows. He slips behind the schoolhouse and behind the gymnasium. Now he walks erect. He is out of danger. The students and the teachers can't see him. He walks toward the wild plum grove beside the Tygart River. "I can understand why the students feel the way they do," thinks Jason as he watches the honey bees flying from one white cluster of wild plum blossoms to another. "This is a terrible time to have to stay inside of four brick walls and study books. This is the time to be alive—the time to be awake! Spring is here! Spring has come to Kentucky's deep valleys. Spring has come to these fair hills!"

Jason stands beneath the plum trees and looks at their boughs. They look as if they were weighted with snow. But it is not snow. The warm April sun beams down from a deep-blue sky to make the plum blossoms look whiter than snow. The bees are alive with sounds as they work among the plum blossoms. The redbirds sing on almost every bough. Jason watches them carrying sticks in their bills. Just as Eustacia said, the rooster birds do the singing while the hen birds work. Jason tries to catch a honey bee by the wing. It escapes him. He tries to catch a polkadot-winged butterfly from the plum blossom. He brushes its wings with his hands but the butterfly sees the shadow of his hand before he grabs for it.

"This is a great time to be out," thinks Jason. "No wonder the students don't want to be in school today. I can see why they want to slip away from the four walls of a house that encloses them and their dreams. Here I am, a man out acting like a small boy. I am playing hooky, too. I am doing the same thing that forty-one students are doing today. I am leaving the high-school office to Eustacia. I'm leaving the teaching to the teachers. Their Principal is out under the wild plum trees—crawling on his hands and knees—trying to catch butterflies and bees. He, too, hates the schoolroom today. He can't lie about it. He has to be honest. He has to tell what is in his heart."

Jason takes a notebook from his pocket. He jots down lines of poetry. The smell of the earth revives him. He sees the beauty in the snow-white clusters of the wild plum blossoms. He hears music in the songs of the birds and the hum of the bees. He feels that the earth beneath him is alive with the white-hair roots of April and the trees above him are filled with the growing green-hair of April. He feels that the earth is alive with music, beauty, and song. This stirs him until he tries to put it down in words. He tries to make the words be alive much as the April about him is alive with growth, beauty, and smell.

The wild plum grove spreads over the east bank of the Tygart River. There is an old road that leads to a farmhouse on the west side of the wild plum grove. Jason crawls toward this old road. He straightens his body and breathes the clean air of April deep into his lungs.

Jason stops as he walks toward the thin tender-leafed water birches and sycamores along the banks of the river. Jason hears a voice down among the water birches. He can hear a voice saying over and over:

"She is as pretty as a percoon flower."

Jason walks toward the sound. He sees a boy sitting at the foot of a water birch. He is looking at the percoon patches on the other side of the river. He has a pencil in his hand and a notebook on his lap. He is thinking. Jason walks closer.

"I have found you, Dick," says Jason. "What are you doing here?"

"Oh, Mr. Stringer," says Dick Martin, "how did you know I was here? Somebody has squealed on me. This is the first time I ever played hooky in my life."

"Are you here alone?" Jason asks.

"I am," says Dick.

Dick is sitting with his back against the water-birch sapling. His feet are propped upon a log.

"Was that you I heard talking to yourself, Dick?" Jason asks.

"I guess it was," says Dick shamefully.

"You were saying, 'She is as pretty as a percoon flower,' weren't you?"

"I was," says Dick. "Look over across the Tygart at the percoon on the bluffs, Mr. Stringer! I can't say that I think a lot about flowers but just somehow they look good to me today. And don't say anything about it—but I'm trying to write a poem,

Mr. Stringer. Gee, but she is as pretty as a percoon flower. This is the first poem I've ever tried to write and I can't get the right word to rhyme with flower."

Dick gets up from behind the water-birch sapling. He crumples the piece of paper in his hand. He throws it on the ground. He picks up his books at the foot of the tree. He puts his pencil in his pocket.

"Your grades are low, Dick," says Jason. "If I suspend you three days from school, you won't be eligible for the Manchester track meet."

"Mr. Stringer, you know that I'm not boasting when I say Mason High School will need me on that day," says Dick. "You know what I'm going to do to Manchester on the dashes. I plan to take five first places in that track meet. You know Big Nick won't take the 440."

"Track meet or no track meet," says Jason Stringer, "I have caught you here, Dick. I have come straight to your hiding place. You can't play hooky and get by with it at Mason High School. You are old enough and big enough to know better."

"Mr. Stringer, don't make it too hard on me," Dick begs. "Just give me a chance to beat Manchester."

"What is all that noise, Dick?" Jason asks.

"Mr. Stringer, you needn't ask me," says Dick. "You know it's time for school to be out and the children are leaving."

"I didn't know," says Jason. "I left my watch at home this morning. This day has slipped by like a shadow."

"It's slipped by for me, too," says Dick.

"I'd better be getting toward the schoolhouse," says Jason.

Dick Martin and Principal Jason Stringer walk up the Tygart River bank. They walk up the old road that leads from the farmhouse. They walk up the road to the tiny path that leads under the thicket of wild plum trees. Jason Stringer gets down on his knees and crawls under the trees. He follows the tiny path. "I have played hooky all day," thinks Jason. "It doesn't seem like it has been three hours since I left the schoolhouse this morning."

"You write poetry, don't you, Mr. Stringer?" Dick asks as they crawl on their hands and knees under the thick mass of wild plum trees.

"It's been a long time since I've written poetry," says Jason. Jason looks at the roof above him. He cannot see the sun through the thick roof of plumtree leaves and the mass of snow-white clusters of wild plum blossoms. "I'll tell you though, Dick," says Jason, "these wild plum blossoms are enough to make a man want to write poetry."

"I'll tell you, Mr. Stringer," says Dick, "I always laughed at students trying to write poetry until this morning. The notion just struck me all of a sudden to go to these woods. Spring had come and something got into my blood. I didn't think you'd find me. I thought I was in a good hiding place."

"I wouldn't have found you," says Jason, "but I heard you trying to write your poem."

"Don't tell that on me," says Dick. "What will the students think of me? They will think I'm a softie. You know I'm not."

"I know you're not, Dick," says Jason Stringer. "You are a good boy in school, Dick. You don't drink, smoke, or chew tobacco. You've always told me the truth. That's why I'm going to make this easy for you."

"Did you ever play hooky, Mr. Stringer?" Dick asks.

"Yes, Dick, I have," says Jason ruefully. "I have played truant many times."

"Then you know how I feel about it."

"Yes."

Dick Martin and Jason Stringer move slowly along under the massive grove of wild plum trees. They keep their heads bent low to miss the wild plum thorns above. Jason leads the way on his hands and knees. Slowly they move under the massive clouds of green and white. Jason crawls from under the wild plum thicket into the open space first. Dick follows him. They stand and brush the dirt from their hands and knees.

"That path is like a rabbit hole," says Dick.

"Yes, it is," says Jason. "You caused me a lot of trouble, Dick. But I found you. You were out writing poetry for a girl. Who was the girl, Dick?"

"Eustacia Pratt," says Dick. "Now don't say anything about that."

"I won't," says Jason.

"Did you ever write poetry for a girl?" Dick asks.

"Yes, for many girls," says Jason.

"And you're not a sissy, Mr. Stringer," says Dick.

"I hope not," says Jason. "What is wrong with writing poetry for your true love in the spring?"

"I don't guess there's anything," says Dick, "but I'll be ineligible for the Manchester track meet now."

"I'll tell you what I'll do, Dick," says Jason. "You gather me enough of these wild plum blossoms to make twenty-one bouquets and bring them to the office. I'll go on to the office now. You bring them to the office. I'll let that be your punishment."

"Gee, Mr. Stringer," says Dick. "I'll be glad to do it. That is great! Then you're not going to suspend me three days!"

"No, I'm not," says Jason.

"I'll never play hooky again." says Dick.

"Now don't say that," says Jason. "You don't know what you will do or you won't do. If April comes again and you're in this high school, you are likely to play hooky again if the day is as pretty as this day has been. This has been a wonderful day."

Eustacia is still waiting in the office when Jason Stringer arrives.

"Mr. Stringer, I've had an awful time today," says Eustacia. "The Superintendent was here to see you. We've telephoned everywhere for you. Several students have been sent to the office. You were not here. I had to send them back. They have gone home now. Mr. Bascom found Kathleen out on the hillside gathering percoon with John Hart. He brought her back to school. I told him you were out hunting students. I didn't know where you were. Professor MacKinney and Miss Burkhardt wanted to see you. I told them you were out and that you said you'd be gone only a short time."

"I'm sorry, Eustacia, that I've caused you waiting all this time," says Jason Stringer. "I haven't been far."

"But I didn't know where to find you," says Eustacia.

"I know you didn't," says Jason. "You couldn't have found me. I was away a million miles from this schoolhouse. I was among the songs of the birds, the lapping of the water, the blowing of the wind, and the smell of wild plum blossoms. I was out among growing things and I forgot about the school. I think I've played hooky today."

"You said you weren't far away from the schoolhouse and then you said you were a million miles away," says Eustacia.

"The Tygart River bank is a million miles away from here today," says Jason. "Eustacia, you take a pair of scissors and cut out each couple's name on a small slip of paper."

Eustacia takes the scissors and cuts each couple's name from the big sheet of paper. Jason looks over the teachers' reports while Eustacia gets the names ready. Before Jason gets the reports checked, before Eustacia gets the names ready, Dick Martin walks before the office window with an armload of wild plum blossoms.

"Here they are, Mr. Stringer," says Dick as he enters the office door. "I have enough for twenty bouquets all right."

Dick's face colors when he looks down at Principal Jason Stringer's desk and sees Eustacia Pratt at work. He lays the plum blossoms on the office desk. Dick does not talk any more. He looks at Eustacia Pratt.

"Dick, you make twenty-one bouquets out of that armload of wild plum blossoms," Jason says. "Eustacia, you put a couple's name on each bouquet as long as the names last."

Dick separates the wild plum blossoms into bouquets. Eustacia smiles as she puts a couple's name on each bouquet. Jason Stringer holds the poetry he has written in the wild plum grove down on his reports.

"We have this done now, Mr. Stringer," says Eustacia. "Is there anything else you want me to do before I leave?"

"Just don't say anything about this," says Jason. "Don't either one of you mention this outside of the school. I'll tell you what I'm going to do. From now on, you students in Mason High School are going to get a spring vacation. It's something we have never had here. We'll have a week's spring vacation about the time the wild plums are in bloom. Tomorrow, I'm going to surprise each couple that played truant. This will be one time when I'm not going to suspend students. I'm going to present each couple with a bouquet. I'll ask the boy to wear it all day with his and his sweetheart's name on it. That will be all the punishment that the students will get."

"Gee, Mr. Stringer," says Dick, "that will hurt them worse than if you'd suspend them from school."

"It won't hurt their grades more, I'm sure," says Jason.

"What do you want done with this extra bouquet, Mr. Stringer?" Eustacia asks.

"That's for Dick," says Jason. "You and Dick are excused now. I have a lot of work I want to stay here to do."

Jason Stringer sits at his desk. He watches Dick and Eustacia leave the school yard. Dick is carrying the bouquet. He watches them as they walk over the hill toward the country road. He watches the young couple until they are out of sight down the long winding road.

from

Newfound

Jim Wayne Miller

I GUESS I didn't spend more than two or three days at home the summer between my junior and senior years at West Madison. I helped George Hawkins haul watermelons from Florida and Georgia. Sometimes I'd get out to Newfound just to pick up clean clothes. Going to sleep by a swamp in Florida, or under a live-oak tree in south Georgia, or loading watermelons at night on a farm where the bitter fragrance of flu-cured tobacco hung on the evening air, I'd think of Newfound Creek and Grandma and Grandpa Smith, Mom and Dad, Jeanette and Eugene, and they would all seem far away, as if they were part of another life I'd lived long ago. I was homesick a little, but when I was, I thought mostly about Selma Austin. When I was a couple of days selling out a load of watermelons at the farmer's market in Mountain City, I'd go by and see Dad, if he happened to be in his office. But mostly I'd lie in the straw in the back of George Hawkins's truck, wait for customers, and listen to country music from the restaurant opposite the market there on Lexington Avenue. Then I thought a lot about Selma.

That summer ended and I started my last year of school. Chinquapins ripened early. On the first Saturday morning after school began, the big prickly burrs on the chinquapin bushes had already turned yellow and burst open, and the chinquapins were shiny black in the morning sunlight. A storm had passed through in the night, but now the air was clear and the mountains seemed to have moved closer. I picked two pockets full of them on the ridge above Grandpa Smith's barn and then walked down the Newfound Creek road toward Austins', hoping to see Selma.

She was sitting at a wooden table under the sycamore tree in the yard, in one of the woven willow chairs the Sutherlands had made, wearing jeans and a pullover, glancing first at an open book, then writing in her notebook. Her little brother Charles Everett crawled about in his playpen at the end of the table. I stepped in behind the big oak tree at the edge of the yard and lobbed a chinquapin at Selma. It bounced on the table beside her; she looked up in the sycamore tree, then started writing again. I lobbed another chinquapin that popped right on the page she was writing on. She looked around. Maybe she saw me draw my arm back. "All right, Robert Wells," she said. "I know you're behind that tree."

I crossed the yard, dragging my feet through the big, crackly sycamore leaves that had already fallen, and sat down at the table beside her. She looked warm and snug in the woolly pullover; her movements as she glanced first at her literature textbook, then at her notebook, were small and quick, like a bird's.

"Sleepyhead, where were you at seven?" I asked.

"I was up at seven, eating breakfast," she said, and went on writing. Selma had a reputation at school for working hard and being smart. If she kept on making good grades, she was sure to get a scholarship to a college.

"I was up, too, but I didn't see you," I said. I'd driven down the road in Grandpa Wells's old farm truck that morning, hauling corn to Tom Davis's mill to be crushed for Grandpa Wells's cattle. I told Selma I'd driven by, trying to sound as if it were something I did every day of my life. The truth was, I hauled the corn just to get to drive Grandpa Wells's truck.

"Did Eugene go with you?" Selma asked. She smiled brightly at Charles Everett, who had pulled up to a standing position and was shaking his playpen violently and babbling, trying to attract her attention. Selma cooed to him.

"No, Eugene's at the house. But he's the only one. Mom and Grandpa and Grandma Smith and Jeanette went to Jewell Hill. They all rode with Carlene Cantrell." I saw the little blue veins in the back of Selma's pretty, smooth hands, and noticed the way her fingers gripped the pencil as she wrote. I had always noticed Selma's hands.

"Tell Eugene not to forget to bring me my history book," she said.

I made the sound of galloping horses on the table with my fingers, and felt disgusted. I had so many tender, heroic things to say to Selma, yet everything came out silly and stupid, like my telling her about hauling corn to mill, while she did her lessons and cooed to her little brother, or worried about her history book. "You want some chinquapins?" I asked.

"No, thanks. They make my tongue sore."

I took hold of the rubber band on her wrist, stretched it, and let it snap back.

"Ouch! Stop that!"

I knew what I was doing was just another stupid thing, but I couldn't keep from doing it. I stretched the rubber band again.

Selma twisted her body around, grabbed my arm with her hand, and dug her sharp fingernails into my wrist. "You'd better let go," she said, her voice rising in warning.

I held on to the rubber band, threatening to let it snap against her wrist.

"All right!" she said, sinking her fingernails deeper, really hurting. Her lips were pressed tightly together, her eyes almost shut, she was gripping so hard.

I drew my arm close to me, and her with it, until she was against me, her lips close to mine, her eyes half-closed. She gasped; I felt her warm breath on my lips. Then she let go of my wrist and I quickly slipped the rubber band off her arm.

"Devil!" she said, patting her brown hair with both hands.

"Devil yourself!" I said, and showed her the deep red crescents her fingernails had made in my wrist. "You ought to be ashamed," I teased. I was very happy at that moment.

"Well, bless his little arm!" she said with mock tenderness, and took my hand gently in both of hers. She raised my obedient hand toward her lips, as if to kiss the red crescents; then, with a diabolical giggle, she cut deep into my wrist with her fingernails again. The deception hurt more than her fingernails.

"Charles Everett, you stop that!" she said, turning from me. Her little brother, down on his hands and knees in the playpen, had reached out through the bars and got a fistful of dried grass and was trying to eat it. Selma smacked his hand, took the grass away from him, and set him in the center of the playpen. "Here, little dirt-dauber, play with your spools."

I picked up one of the spools, cut notches on both ends with my knife, then cut a couple of little twigs from a low-hanging limb, and with the spool, the twigs, and the rubber band, I made Selma's little brother a tractor. I wound it up, set it on the floor of the playpen, and let it creep toward him. He sat very still watching it. "Tractor," I said. Charles Everett waved his arms excitedly and tried to say tractor.

I wound the tractor again, turned to Selma, and put it down on her shoulder. The tractor started creeping on the woolly green pullover. She drew her head down, turning to Charles Everett. "Make him stop, Charles Everett. Robert is a bigger baby than you are." Her little brother waved his arms and babbled. She wound the tractor up, set it down in his playpen, and picked up her pencil again.

Suddenly I realized that Selma surely knew I didn't come by to sit in the yard with her because I liked to flip rubber bands or make spool tractors for her little brother. Maybe she didn't know how I had thought about her all summer, in Florida, in Georgia, in South Carolina, but surely she must know I liked her, loved her. "I have to write an essay," I sighed, watching her write.

"What on?"

"Love," I lied. Actually, Mr. Bennett, my English teacher, had said we could write about anything that had happened to us during the summer, or about anything we thought was worth writing about.

Selma bent down again to wind the tractor for Charles Everett. I disliked her little brother. Every time I came to the brink of saying something to Selma that I really wanted to say—not just stupid, silly stuff—her little brother did something to distract her. I threw a chinquapin against the oak tree—so hard the chinquapin bounded halfway back into the yard. "I'd better go get started on that essay," I said, and walked off through the noisy leaves.

"Tell Eugene when he's through with my—"

"Yeah, I will." I walked away, throwing chinquapins high into the deep, blue sky, remembering painfully how Selma had started to kiss my wrist, then dug in with her fingernails.

I came around the side of the hill, through the stubby lespedeza, and stopped at the corner of the barn when I saw Eugene standing on the kitchen porch, stripped to the waist, his back to me. For a minute I couldn't figure what he was doing. Then I saw the aluminum pan on the worktable and the towel hanging over the edge of the table. Eugene was shaving—or trying to. He was looking into the mirror and the reflection of the razor was confusing him, for he kept changing his grip on it, trying to discover the right way to hold it.

I started to turn away, for I didn't want Eugene to think I had been standing there watching him shave for the first time—although that was exactly what I had been doing. He must have felt my presence, because he turned, his face covered with so much lather he looked like Santa Claus, and saw me. I came on into the backyard and climbed the steps up to the kitchen porch, trying to act as if Eugene were doing the most ordinary thing in the world.

"Lots of chinquapins this year," I said. "I got my pockets full in a few minutes."

Eugene pinched the tip of his nose and carefully shaved his upper lip. The razor didn't make a sound. "That so?" he said when he had finished with his upper lip.

I went on talking about chinquapins, telling him where every chinquapin bush in the whole county was, while Eugene said he knew, or didn't know, where those bushes were, or else he just grunted. I guess he must have thought I was crazy to stand there for fifteen minutes and talk about nothing but chinquapins. All I was trying to do was keep him from being embarrassed by standing there, without saying something smart about his shaving for the first time.

He finished, splashed water on his face, and dried with the towel. I glanced secretly at his face, and it was as if I had never seen him before. Eugene was fifteen now, and his face was strangely different; and yet it was the same difference I had often noticed in boys' faces. I wouldn't see them all summer, and then when I saw them again after school started in the fall, they'd be different. I guess the same thing had happened to me, but I hadn't noticed it about myself.

I hadn't seen Eugene all summer, and now it had happened to him. The baby roundness of his face had hardened into definite planes and angles; his jaw was firmer, his nose more prominent and slightly curved, instead of just being a button. In that secret glance that caught only the outline of his face, I saw the change, saw what he would look like as a man. I looked more closely, and the difference seemed to fade, then come again. I thought Eugene looked a little like the faces of our people in the oval picture frames down at Grandma and Grandpa Wells's and on the wall here at Grandma and Grandpa Smith's.

"Have some chinquapins," I said quickly, when I became aware that I was staring at him. I gave him a handful. Now Eugene looked like the face in the old tintype, the one Grandma Smith found behind the picture of our great-grandfather Leland.

"Thanks. Maybe I'll go up on the ridge this afternoon and pick some, too. Pay you back."

I followed Eugene through the kitchen and back to our room, where I got Mom's little portable typewriter, the one she had practiced at home with. I carried the typewriter out to the porch, where I sat down to write my essay. I sat a long time trying to decide what to write about. There were so many things. I could write about all the trips I'd made hauling watermelons that summer. But all I could think of was Eugene's face, and Selma, sitting at the table in her yard, studying and babysitting her little brother. I wondered if she would still be there when I drove past later in the afternoon, bringing the crushed corn from the mill in Grandpa Wells's old farm truck. Then I remembered the Sutherlands and decided to write about them. I wrote a while, went into the kitchen and made a sandwich, came back out on the porch, and went on writing.

It was almost two o'clock, and I was retyping my essay when Eugene came out on the porch. He had already been up on the ridge picking chinquapins, and he had both pockets full. He stood on the porch a minute, then went back into the house; I heard him pulling out drawers and slamming them shut again. A minute later he came out on the kitchen porch and asked me if I knew where Mom kept her needles. I told him. He went back inside, clomped out a few minutes later, and stood with his thumbs hooked in the top of his beltless jeans, watching me type. "Can I have a piece of fishing line off your reel?"

"How much?"

"Not much. Just a little. Two feet?"

"Sure. What do you want it for?"

"I need a piece." He went back inside.

I finished copying what I had written and took my notebook back to our room. I tried to open the door, but it was latched from the inside. Eugene came to the door and unlatched it. I put my notebook down and started back out. Eugene was tinkering with the lock. "Must be something wrong with it," he said, turning the knob back and forth. He popped a chinquapin into his mouth.

"Selma said for you to bring her her history book when you're through with it."

Eugene snapped his fingers, chewed a minute. He picked up the book and fell across the bed with it. "I've not even started to read it," he said.

I paused in the door, not knowing where to go or what to do. I had the feeling there was something I had intended to say to Eugene, but I must have forgotten it. I went down and waited on the porch. It was very quiet with Mom, Jeanette, and Grandma and Grandpa Smith gone to Jewell Hill with Carlene Cantrell, and Eugene lying on the bed reading. The whole day had been strange: first, walking down to Grandpa Wells's in the early morning chill and hauling corn to mill in his truck; then picking chinquapins on the ridge and sitting with Selma; noticing Eugene's face; and now this stillness, the deep blue sky, bright sun, the puffs of milkweed floating through the air, and the rustling of leaves in the trees in the yard when a breeze stirred—like a far-off waterfall. It seemed that everything was changing; everything stayed a little while, then passed on, like Newfound School, or the Sutherlands, or bees that decided, mysteriously, to leave a hive and fly away in a dark cloud.

Carlene brought Mom, Jeanette, and Grandma and Grandpa Smith home about three-thirty. (Mom still hadn't learned to drive.) I helped them carry shopping bags into the house. Grandpa Smith had bought two bales of barbed wire. We lifted them carefully out of the trunk of Carlene Cantrell's old Chevrolet, then carried them to the barn by running a crowbar through the hole in the bale.

Later I walked back down to Grandpa Wells's, got his truck, and drove to the mill to pick up the sacks of crushed corn. I drove slowly along the dusty gravel road. When I got to the mill, Tom Davis, the miller, his ears white with cornmeal dust, shouted to me over the roar of the mill that my sacks wouldn't be ready for at least an hour. I paced up and down in front of the mill. But there was no way to hurry Tom Davis. I got in Grandpa Wells's truck and drove over to the old blacksmith shop, where I'd seen some cars parked as I'd come down the road. J. D. Marler, Mack Woody, and some more boys were playing blackjack for pennies. I played for a while and lost all the pennies I had.

It was after five when I got the sacks loaded and started back with them. Selma probably wouldn't be out in the yard this late. But she might be. No, she probably wouldn't be. I whipped around the turn: she was. And Eugene had come to bring her history book. I turned off the road and pulled down the Austins' drive, cut the switch at the edge of the yard, and walked across to where they were sitting at the table under the sycamore tree.

Selma had brought out cake and milk for her and Eugene; they were sitting at the table nibbling cake, their heads together over the history book. "Hi," Selma said, without looking up. I stood behind them and peered over Eugene's shoulder, pretending to look at the open book. But I was really looking at the chinquapin necklace Selma was wearing—the kind Jeanette always made. I stood there behind Selma and Eugene, and saw that the chinquapins were strung on my black fishing line.

"What did you say for number fourteen?" Selma asked Eugene.

I popped a chinquapin into my mouth, cracked it open, and stood there pushing the meaty center out of the hull with the tip of my tongue. Selma's little brother Charles Everett threw his spool tractor out of the playpen, then reached through the bars for it, but it was too far away. He gathered a fistful of dry grass; very carefully and thoughtfully he began stuffing the grass into his mouth. Selma didn't even notice.

Barbara Allen

compiled by Mellinger Edward Henry

Way down South where I came from
Is where I got my learning.
I fell in love with a pretty little girl,
And her name is Barbey Ellen.

I courted her for seven years,
And I asked her if she would marry.
With a bowed down head and a sweet little smile,
She never made no answer.

Early along in the spring,
When the red roses were blooming,
A young man on his death bed lay
For the love of Barbey Ellen.

He sent his servant to the town
To a place where she was dwelling:
"My master is love-sick and sent for you,
If your name is Barbey Ellen."

She slightly talked and slowly walked
And slowly went unto him.
"Young man, young man, I heard you were sick,
For the love of me, your darling."

"Yes, I am sick, and very sick
And with me death is dwelling
And none the better will I be,
Till I get Barbey Ellen."

"Yes, you are sick, and very sick,
And with you death is dwelling,
But none the better will you be
While my name is Barbey Ellen.

"Don't you remember the other day
When we were all a-drinking,
You passed the glass to the ladies all around,
But you slighted me, your darling?"

"Yes, I remember the other day,
When we were all a-drinking:
I passed the glass to the ladies all around,
But all for you, my darling."

He turned his pale face to the wall,
His back he turned towards them:
"Adieu, adieu, to all this world,
But be kind to Barbey Ellen."

She had not rode five miles from town,
Till she heard the death bells ringing,
And every lick, it seemed to strike:
"Hard hearted Barbey Ellen."

She looked east, she looked west,
Till she saw the pale corpse coming:
"Lay him down, lay him down,
And let me look upon him."

The more she looked, the worse she got
Till she bursted out in crying:
"Young man, young man, you died for me.
I will die for you tomorrow."

They buried Sweet Willie in one church yard,
And Barbey in the other,
And out of Barbey's breast sprang a red, red rose,
And out of his a brier.

They grew and grew to such a length of height,
Till they could not grow no higher;
And there they tied in a true-lover's knot
And the rose run around the brier.

Why Can't I Take Love Easy?

compiled by Mildred Haun

Why can't I take love easy
As the leaves upon the tree?
They only fade and wither.
So is his love for me.

Chorus
I don't know why I love him.
For he does not care for me.
But still my mind will wonder
Wherever he may be.

He is just as nice as a flower.
But he does not care for me.
But still I'll always love him
Wherever he may be.

He may go across the ocean.
He may go across the sea.
He may travel this wide world
over.
He'll never find another like
me.

An April Day

Joseph S. Cotter, Jr.

On such a day as this I think,
    On such a day as this,
When earth and sky and nature's whole
    Are clad in April's bliss;
And balmy zephyrs gently waft
    Upon your cheek a kiss;
Sufficient is it just to live
    On such a day as this.

Memories

Joseph S. Cotter, Jr.

The burnished glow of the old-gold moon
    Shines brightly over me.
A thousand stars, like a thousand isles
    In a dark and placid sea,
Bring memories of a golden night,
    Bedecked in Autumn's hue
And fragrant with the lilac's bloom,
    That brought me joy—and you.

Hardweed Path Going

A. R. Ammons

Every evening, down into the hardweed
going,
the slop bucket heavy, held-out, wire handle
freezing in the hand, put it down a minute, the jerky
smooth unspilling levelness of the knees,
meditation of a bucket rim,
lest the wheat meal,
floating on clear greasewater, spill,
down the grown-up path:

don't forget to slop the hogs,
feed the chickens,
water the mule,
cut the kindling,
build the fire,
call up the cow:

supper is over, it's starting to get
dark early,
better get the scraps together, mix a little meal in,
nothing but swill.

The dead-purple woods hover on the west.
I know those woods.
Under the tall, ceiling-solid pines, beyond the edge of
field and brush, where the wild myrtle grows,
I let my jo-reet loose.
A jo-reet is a bird. Nine weeks of summer he
sat on the well bench in a screened box,
a stick inside to walk on,
"jo-reet," he said, "jo-reet."
and I
would come up to the well and draw the bucket down
deep into the cold place where red and white marbled
clay oozed the purest water, water celebrated
throughout the country:

"Grits all gone?"
"jo-reet."
Throw a dipper of cold water on him. Reddish-black
flutter.
"reet, reet, reet!"
Better turn him loose before
cold weather comes on.
Doom caving in
inside
any pleasure, pure
attachment
of love.

Beyond the wild myrtle away from cats I turned him loose
and his eye asked me what to do, where to go;
he hopped around, scratched a little, but looked up at me.
Don't look at me. Winter is coming.
Disappear in the bushes. I'm tired of you and will
be alone hereafter. I will go dry in my well.
I will turn still.
Go south. Grits is not available in any natural form.
Look under leaves, try mushy logs, the floors of pinywoods.
South into the dominion of bugs.

They're good woods.
But lay me out if a mourning dove far off in the dusky pines
starts.

Down the hardweed path going,
leaning, balancing, away from the bucket, to
Sparkle, my favorite hog, sparse, fine black hair,
grunted while feeding if rubbed,
scratched against the hair, or if talked to gently:
got the bottom of the slop bucket:
"Sparkle . . .
You hungry?
Hungry, girly?"
blowing, bubbling in the trough.

Waiting for the first freeze:

"Think it's going to freeze tonight?" say the neighbors,
the neighbors, going by.

Hog-killing.

Oh, Sparkle, when the axe tomorrow morning falls
and the rush is made to open your throat,

I will sing, watching dry-eyed as a man, sing my
love for you in the tender feedings.

She's nothing but a hog, boy.

Bleed out, Sparkle, the moon-chilled bleaches
of your body hanging upside-down
hardening through the mind and night of the first freeze.

The Fish

Joe Survant

The fish hangs
in the heavy breath of the water
swelling.
We laid many traps
drifting carefully downstream.
That night I felt her,
slow and heavy on the line.
We took her out in the dark
holding her tight by the hair,
not noticing her hard scales
like old armor,
and hurried back
shouting our trophy—
"What a great fish we have caught!"
And I saw by the light that double life
flopping and gasping by the fire
with two human eyes.
Stunned,
I watched
while they began
with a knife
to scrape off those
great silver scales.

Squirrel Stand

Jim Wayne Miller

Now burley's curing in the high-tiered barn
and yellow leaves ride out on slow black water.
Cold wind moving in the rows of corn
rattles the blades like an old man pulling fodder.
Down from the mountain pastures overnight,
cattle stand by the yellow salt block bawling.
Now it's September in the world; fine rain is falling.

—When gray squirrels had grown fat on hickory nuts,
my gun in the crook of my arm, once I went stepping
through yellow leaves and fine rain falling.
Resting on a ridge above our tents,
I heard what raincrows off in the mist were calling:
my days were growing full, sliding, dropping
like waterbeads along the barbed-wire fence.

The Far and the Near

Thomas Wolfe

ON the outskirts of a little town upon a rise of land that swept back from the railway there was a tidy little cottage of white boards, trimmed vividly with green blinds. To one side of the house there was a garden neatly patterned with plots of growing vegetables, and an arbor for the grapes that ripened late in August. Before the house there were three mighty oaks which sheltered it in their clean and massive shade in summer, and to the other side there was a border of gay flowers. The whole place had an air of tidiness, thrift, and modest comfort.

Every day, a few minutes after two o'clock in the afternoon, the limited express between two cities passed this spot. At that moment, the great train, having halted for a breathing space at the town near by, was beginning to lengthen evenly into its stroke, but it had not yet reached the full drive of its terrific speed. It swung into view deliberately, swept past with a powerful swaying motion of the engine, a low smooth rumble of its heavy cars upon pressed steel, and then it vanished into the cut. For a moment the progress of the engine could be marked by heavy bellowing puffs of smoke that burst at spaced intervals above the edges of the meadow grass, and finally nothing could be heard but the solid clacking tempo of the wheels receding into the drowsy stillness of the afternoon.

Every day for more than twenty years, as the train had approached this house, the engineer had blown on the whistle, and every day, as soon as she heard this signal, a woman had appeared on the back porch of the little house and waved to him. At first she had a small child clinging to her skirts, and now this child had grown to full womanhood, and every day she, too, came with her mother to the porch and waved.

The engineer had grown old and gray in the service. He had driven his great train, loaded with its weight of lives, across the land ten thousand times. His own children had grown up and married, and four times he had seen before him on the tracks the ghastly dot of tragedy converging like a cannon ball to its eclipse of horror at the boiler head—a light spring wagon filled with children, with its clustered row of small stunned faces; a cheap automobile stalled upon the tracks, set with the wooden figures of people paralyzed with fear; a battered hobo walking by the rail, too deaf and old to hear the whistle's warning; and a form flung past his window with a scream—all this the man had seen and known. He had known all the grief, the joy, the peril, and the labor such a man could know; he had grown seamed and weathered in his loyal service, and now, schooled by the qualities of faith and courage and humbleness that attended his labor, he had grown old, and had the grandeur and wisdom that these men have.

But no matter what peril or tragedy he had known, the vision of the little house and the women waving to him with a brave free motion of the arm had become fixed in the mind of the engineer as something beautiful and enduring, something beyond all change and ruin, and something that would always be the same, no matter what mishap, grief, or error might break the iron schedule of his days.

The sight of the little house and of these two women gave him the most extraordinary happiness he had ever known. He had seen them in a thousand lights, a hundred weathers. He had seen them through the harsh bare light of wintry gray across the brown and frosted stubble of the earth, and he had seen them again in the green luring sorcery of April.

He felt for them and for the little house in which they lived such tenderness as a man might feel for his own children, and at length the picture of their lives was carved so sharply in his heart that he felt that he knew their lives completely, to every hour and moment of the day, and he resolved that one day, when his years of service should be ended, he would go and find these people and speak at last with them whose lives had been so wrought into his own.

That day came. At last the engineer stepped from a train onto the station platform of the town where these two women lived. His years upon the rail had ended. He was a pensioned servant of his company, with no more work to do. The engineer walked slowly through the station and out into the streets of the town. Everything was as strange to him as if he had never seen this town before. As he walked on, his sense of bewilderment and confusion grew. Could this be the town he had passed ten thousand times? Were these the same houses he had seen so often from the high windows of his cab? It was all as unfamiliar, as disquieting as a city in a dream, and the perplexity of his spirit increased as he went on.

Presently the houses thinned into the straggling outposts of the town, and the street faded into a country road—the one on which the women lived. And the man plodded on slowly in the heat and dust. At length he stood before the house he sought. He knew at once that he had found the proper place. He saw the lordly oaks before the house, the flower beds, the garden and the arbor, and farther off, the glint of rails.

Yes, this was the house he sought, the place he had passed so many times, the destination he had longed for with such happiness. But now that he had found it, now that he was here, why did his hand falter on the gate; why had the town, the road, the earth, the very entrance to this place he loved, turned unfamiliar as the landscape of some ugly dream? Why did he feel this sense of confusion, doubt, and hopelessness?

At length he entered by the gate, walked slowly up the path, and in a moment more had mounted three short steps that led up to the porch, and was knocking on the door. Presently he heard steps in the hall, the door was opened, and a woman stood facing him.

And instantly, with a sense of bitter loss and grief, he was sorry he had come. He knew at once that the woman who stood there looking at him with a mistrustful eye was the same woman who had waved to him so many thousand times. But her face was harsh and pinched and meager; the flesh sagged wearily in sallow folds, and the small eyes peered at him with timid suspicion and uneasy doubt. All the brave freedom, the warmth and the affection that he had read into her gesture, vanished in the moment that he saw her and heard her unfriendly tongue.

And now his own voice sounded unreal and ghastly to him as he tried to explain his presence, to tell her who he was and the reason he had come. But he faltered on, fighting stubbornly against the horror of regret, confusion, disbelief that surged up in his spirit, drowning all his former joy and making his act of hope and tenderness seem shameful to him.

At length the woman invited him almost unwillingly into the house, and called her daughter in a harsh shrill voice. Then, for a brief agony of time, the man sat in an ugly little parlor, and he tried to talk while the two women stared at him with a dull, bewildered hostility, a sullen, timorous restraint.

And finally, stammering a crude farewell, he departed. He walked away down the path and then along the road toward town, and suddenly he knew that he was an old man. His heart, which had been brave and confident when it looked along the familiar vista of the rails, was now sick with doubt and horror as it saw the strange and unsuspected visage of the earth which had always been within a stone's throw of him, and which he had never seen or known. And he knew that all the magic of that bright lost way, the vista of that shining line, the imagined corner of that small good universe of hope's desire, could never be got again.

from

A Conversation with Robert Penn Warren

Bill Moyers

edited by Floyd C. Watkins and John T. Hiers

This excerpt, taken from Bill Moyers' conversation with Warren, was taped at Yale University in 1976.

WARREN. There's something in the modern world going on, and I don't profess to understand it. We can make guesses about it.

MOYERS. Make some guesses.

WARREN. Well, we are, for one thing—the whole Western world is undergoing some deep change in its very nature in what it can believe in. And one of those things is clearly how democracy can function in a world of technology. That's one thing. Another thing, it just seems the massive number of people involved. Government's designed, the modern liberal democracy is designed, to function within a certain limited world.

MOYERS. How successful do you think we are in keeping some notion of democracy, and some concept of the self alive in a highly technological, scientific age of huge organizations?

WARREN. Not successful enough. I think you can see many indications of that.

MOYERS. What are some of the manifestations you see that deeply trouble you?

WARREN. Now, this is a small academic matter in one sense: the death of history.

MOYERS. The death of history?

WARREN. Yes. History departments are on the decline, I'm told. I don't know the statistics. But certainly they . . . the sense of the past is passing out of the consciousness of the generation.

MOYERS. What do you think will be the consequence of that?

WARREN. I don't know how you can have a future without a sense of the past. A real future. And we have a book like Plumb's book, *The Death of the Past*, which is a very impressive and disturbing book. As Plumb puts it, in the past people have tried and learned what wisdom they could from history. They have tried to learn from what has happened before. Now, he says, social science will take the place of history. And the past will die . . . and the machine will take over . . . done by social scientists. That's his prediction. He says only history keeps alive the human sense, history in the broadest sense of the word. It might be literary history or political history or any other kind of history. It's man's long effort to be human. And if a student understands this or tries to penetrate this problem, he becomes human. If he once gives that up as a concern, he turns to mechanism.

MOYERS. The machine.

WARREN. The machine.

MOYERS. Process?

WARREN. Some process to take charge. Now he may have . . . there are many kinds of machines, there're many kinds of processes he can turn to. But the . . . the sense of a human being's effort to be human and to somehow develop his humanity, that is what history's about.

MOYERS. Do you sense among the students you teach, and among the young people you know, this loss of the past, this disconnection from history?

WARREN. Yes, I have. I have indeed.

MOYERS. What is the effect of it?

WARREN. It's a certain kind of blankness. A certain kind of blankness. But the past is dead for a great number of young people; it just doesn't exist.

MOYERS. I know you once wrote that Americans felt liberated from time, and that it gave them a sense of being, gave us a sense of being on a great gravy train with a first-class ticket.

WARREN. Well, we had the country of the future, the party of the future . . . we had the future ahead of us, and we had this vast space behind us on this continent. We had time and space. We could change the limitations of the European world. Such a simple thing as a man's hands becoming valuable. A man on the American continent in the eighteenth century was valuable, neighbors were valuable, hands were valuable, there were things for hands to do. And so the whole sense of the human value changed . . . right . . . beginning with the value of hands, what they could do. Or the value of a neighbor down the road a mile away instead of twenty miles away. These things made a whole difference in the sense of life. And it's a fundamental stimulus to our sense of our own destiny.

MOYERS. They also were a power incentive, were they not, to human dignity?

WARREN. To human dignity because the hands mean something. They're not just things owned by somebody else. They belong to that man. And then, all of the rest of the factors that enter into the creation of American . . . the American spirit. All of those things are involved.

MOYERS. You said once . . .

WARREN. We could always move, and the sense of time—being time-bound and space-bound—disappeared, but mitigated, anyway. A whole psychology was born; it'd never been in the world before.

MOYERS. A very optimistic philosophy of progress.

WARREN. That's right. As Jefferson said, in writing to his daughter Martha, he said, Americans—I think it was his daughter Martha, anyway—Americans fear nothing, you see, cannot be overcome by earnest application, you see, and what's the other word? Ingenuity.

MOYERS. Ingenuity.

WARREN. Americans assume that there are no insoluble problems.

MOYERS. We've really been—we've really been trapped, in a sense, by Thomas Jefferson's definitions of America in those terms, haven't we?

WARREN. That's right, we assume that we can solve anything rather easily. And we're always right. We think we're usually right about it. Since we can solve things, we're the ones who are right.

MOYERS. I remember you wrote once that America was defined by one man in an upstairs room. Thomas Jefferson writing "all men are created equal," giving this great metaphysical boost to the American self-image.

WARREN. Yes, he gave more than any one person, gave us our self-image. I think he was wrong about human nature in his emphasis on it. He wasn't a fool, of course; he knew that there were bad people. He knew there were stupid people because of six, I think, siblings in his outfit. Four had something wrong with them in the head. And the other one died young. Jefferson's genius was the only one of this brood of children who was even—I think this is right now—who was not in some way deficient. And so he was probably aware of the fact that all men are not born equal, right there at his own fireside.

MOYERS. How do people who still live with that mystique of democracy, that mystique of the self, how do they come to terms with the world you have described as being large, impersonal, driven by science and technology?

WARREN. They say that's the way to solve it, by and large. They say somebody will fix it up, the expert will fix it up some way. The magic cancer cure, there'll be this, there'll be that. The expert will come along and fix it up. And our faith has gone from God to experts. And sometimes experts don't work out.

MOYERS. Well, you've written a lot about how to hold on to the sense of self when the world is changing this way. What do you say when the world enforces a beating upon us from many directions, forces we can't understand, forces we can't change, forces we can't even define? How do you . . . ?

WARREN. Some forces we don't . . . even want to change; we want our technology and we should have it, should want it. It's how we use it, that's important. It's the attitude toward it, it seems to me is important, not its presence. From scientific speculation to the applications in technology represents a great human achievement. It's how we approach this and how we wish to use it.

MOYERS. Well, I wouldn't want to abandon, would you, this material progress we've made, the things that make life so much more amenable.

WARREN. God, no, I don't want to abandon it. My grandfather said he took a very dim view of the modern world—he was born in '38.

MOYERS. Eighteen thirty-eight . . .

WARREN. Eighteen thirty-eight, and fought the Civil War and wound up life as . . . he died in 1919, 1920, something like that—'21. He looked around the modern world and found it not all to his taste. But he said they have got two things that make it worthwhile. Fly screens and painless dentistry. Well, I'm for fly screens and painless dentistry too. I want that and I want some other things to boot.

MOYERS. What is the proper posture or attitude from all the years you've lived?

WARREN. The problem is finally a human problem, and not a technical problem. And we're back to the history again. The sense of the human as being the key sense. As we talk about education, this means the so-called humanities is the only place for students to find the point of reference for the application of their science and their technology. That is the sense of the struggle to define values.

MOYERS. What are the values that are most important to you now?

WARREN. Well, I can tell you what my pleasures are.

MOYERS. What are your pleasures?

WARREN. Put it this way. Because I'm selfish and want to fill my days in a way that pleases me. Well, it so happens that my chief interest in life, aside from my friendly affections and family affections, which is another thing—though they're related—is the fact I like novels and poems, as I want to read them and I want to write them . . . as I have an occupation which to me . . . I can go beyond that—now, why that occupation? It's the only way that I can try to make sense to myself of my own experience . . . is this way. Otherwise I feel rather lost . . . in the ruck of my experience and the experience I observe around me. If you write a poem or read the poem—somebody else has written one that suits you, that pleases you, this is a way of making your own life make sense to you. It's your way of trying to give shape to experience. And the satisfaction of living is feeling that you're living significantly.

MOYERS. Does it . . . ?

WARREN. That doesn't mean grandly; that means it has a meaning, it has a shape, that your life is not being wasted, it isn't just being from this to that.

MOYERS. It also means imposing . . .

WARREN. And understanding.

MOYERS. . . . and imposing order, doesn't it?

WARREN. Order.

MOYERS. Some sense of order.

WARREN. Some sense of order on it, yes.

MOYERS. What does poetry and literature offer people in an age of technology and science?

WARREN. I say it offers an inward landscape. Now, I've been talking about outer landscape, but it offers an inner landscape . . . it offers a sense of what man is like inside. What experience is like, he can see perspectives of experience. This may be in poetry or it may be in history or it may be in political science; it may be taken in historical perspective. Man's view of how he should govern himself over a period of time has changed.

MOYERS. But how does it help us to see ways to deal with technology, with organization, with size?

WARREN. It makes us ask the question how that light or this object or this automobile or this plane will serve our deepest human needs. Or whether it's a gadget, whether it's a toy. Now, when Coleridge has the Ancient Mariner shoot the albatross for no reason except he has a crossbow to shoot the albatross, he's dealing with that problem. The problem was already there, you see. A machine defines the act. The man shoots the bird only because he has a crossbow. Why should he shoot the bird? He has no reason to shoot the bird. It's a gratuitous act. The machine defines the act. Because the machine will do so-and-so, therefore it must be done. See what I'm getting at there? Coleridge's poem is a criticism . . . man as victim of technology.

MOYERS. How do we get control?

WARREN. It's a constant struggle. It means trying to inspect the things that shape us, that make us. Once we understand it, we can sometimes do something about it.

All That Glisters Isn't Gold

Doris Betts

WHEN I was a little girl, before the term "babysitter" had been invented, I used to stay with Miss Carrie whenever my parents were going places. Now that I think about it, I wonder where they went and what they did—but I never wondered then. Certain days I would be taken to Miss Carrie's house on Ingram Street. About the time all the possibilities of her house, yard, and possessions had been exhausted, my mother would arrive to take me home.

There was an odor in Miss Carrie's house, hard to identify. If you put your face close to a plate of cold leftover biscuits and breathed in deeply . . . Not exactly that odor, but it would be close enough. When I came home I would stand in the hall and try to discover the smell of my own house, but I never could.

With Miss Carrie lived her twenty-three-year-old nephew Granville, whom she had reared like a son for family reasons. Miss Carrie worried about Granville, who had gone off to the university in Chapel Hill and learned to be an atheist. She worried out loud and in his presence. I worried silently, because I loved Granville and I wasn't sure love was permitted atheists.

All the time Granville kept arguing religion with my mother and his Aunt Carrie. Anybody could tell by their voices his arguments were better than theirs.

My mother might say, her tone defensive, "You been to college and can *talk* good, but the Lord looketh on the inner man!"

The talk would go on and on: Granville speaking and explaining and making his points, and my mother quoting. And Granville asking long, serious, involved questions; and my mother reciting.

If Granville was uptown in his new insurance office, my mother would comfort Miss Carrie and give her advice. "Don't you argue with Granville your own self. You let the Lord do that. That's why we've got Scripture."

I lay on my stomach under the bed. Even the dust on the linoleum was cold.

"I want you to know, even a little child can ask some hard questions!" my mother sighed. I smiled proudly and let my finger travel the long closing spiral of the bedspring overhead.

It was not necessary that I listen to Mother's side of these planning sessions with Miss Carrie. Long since I'd heard all these things. By now I could say great chunks of catechism and memory work, could duplicate my mother's faith in the mirror of repetition. I had been taught all the references available to doubters. I knew the way to open a good Christian discussion with any atheist was to announce, "In the beginning was the Word, and the Word was with God, and the Word . . ." Some days I hoped this made more sense to atheists than it did to me.

So it was not necessary that I listen to the two women as they ran through their review, in preparation for Granville's test. Those words lay in me so precise and long familiar I never thought of them any more than I noticed my fingernails. I found a hairpin under the bed and began to scrape old dirt from between the boards in the corner.

I knew everything my mother and Miss Carrie would say; but where did Granville learn *his* words? In what class had those strange verses been taught? Sharp words, hostile ones, words that built up some sort of idea tower and then toppled it down like Babel, keen words—yet for all their edge they fell from him lightly, as if it were not hard work to blaspheme.

Each of his words was like a splinter and each slid invisibly inside me. There was a sore spot wherever one had penetrated; soon there were bruises all over my religion it was not safe to touch. I preferred the soreness from those splinters to the painful operation of having them removed.

My mother sometimes complained that if Granville was home when I spent the day at Miss Carrie's I later had a restless night and tended to fever; but I think she only said this so she could add, obliquely, "By their fruits ye shall know them." And nudge my daddy, who was Granville's friend.

Whenever my mother brought me to Miss Carrie's we usually found her sitting in an armless rocker on her front porch, behind a jungle of fern and geranium plants. Neither my parents nor Granville nor Miss Carrie owned an automobile, so it always seemed to be summer when we set out on foot for the three blocks to her house on Ingram Street. Miss Carrie owned seventeen fat clay pots of geraniums and eight more of fern which she kept on her porch from April to October. Every bright day these were moved off their regular shelves onto the steps and along the front railing to catch the sunlight, and twice a day each was watered out of an antique blue cream pitcher which held just the right amount. Twenty-five trips old Miss Carrie made from her kitchen night and morning, rather than bring out one big bucket to dip from. It made her appreciate things, she said.

Miss Carrie would part the fern fronds as we came up her walk and say with surprise, "Now look who's here!" even though everything had been prearranged.

Courtesy required that my mother sit on the porch awhile with Miss Carrie. She figured this into her schedule before we set out from home—how long to walk, how long to sit and talk. A hundred times now she repeated to me the rules of good behavior she had already told me on the way, while exchanging news with Miss Carrie and admiring the ferns. I rolled around on the front yard's mounds of summer grass with its texture of pine needles, never mowed, which simply grew longer and tougher and leaned over and covered the ground in lumps. Sometimes Miss Carrie would lead her old cow up from the barn and stake her in the front yard. You could hear front doors slamming up and down the whole block of Ingram Street.

At last Mother would leave and I would move to the porch steps and hand Miss Carrie her spit can each time the snuff juice swelled too far, and pretend to listen while she complained about the neighbors behind those closed front doors. Miss Carrie did not get along with any of her neighbors. To hear her tell it, it was rotten luck the only nice people in town lived along different streets. All this was ritual and never varied.

Finally she'd say, "Want something to eat?" She emptied her mouth into the can, spilling some down the red tomato label. And we would go inside.

First I took a deep breath of that biscuit odor, then peeked left into the front room, where I was never allowed to play. That room was dark—dust motes ascended and descended before its only window—and on the floor was a mustard-colored fabric rug instead of the usual linoleum. There was one worn sofa which my daddy said had been manufactured without any springs in the seat.

In one far corner stood a huge roll-top desk, always closed and locked. My daddy said Yes, that wooden part would really roll up out of sight, but I didn't see how there was room. A floor lamp with a fringed shade was placed near the desk, and in the other far corner leaned a single crutch—just the lone crutch. Evey time I passed the door into the front room, I watched for it. ("Granville borrowed that once, I think," Miss Carrie once answered me. What kind of sense did that make?)

Last of all, beside the hard sofa there was some stringed instrument. I think it must have been a mandolin; and yet how in the world could it have been a mandolin! Like everything else in the room, whatever-that-was could never be touched. I always had to see it from the hall. I never heard it make a tune.

Past that door and down the hall we went into the back room where all the living and eating were done. Here Miss Carrie and I ate bread and milk off an enormous oval table, saying nothing. Then I would be sent outdoors to play.

What Miss Carrie called "play" was work for me, since each time I came I cleaned out the lily pond beside her house. Probably she never knew I cleaned it. The routine was a game and a self-imposed duty. I itched to get the bread and milk swallowed and run out to the pond.

It was really no pond, only a big barrel buried in the ground with rocks heaped around its rim. The water which filled it to the edge was rank and stagnant and crowded with rotting lily pads. Around the edge, like a layer of paint, was a green scum which sometimes bubbled.

The pond had been lost until the first time I came to visit Miss Carrie. It had entirely vanished under a matting of vines and weeds and old lilies. I would never have guessed a pool was there had she not shown me the place. "Don't fall in there," she called in her cracked voice. I poked through the leafy net and my fingers fell into the shock of cold water.

"Used to fish," said Miss Carrie. "Kept my minnows there."

I knew it was impossible she had ever been young enough to *fish!* But, after the first discovery, the deserted pond was mine. Between visits it would often grow shut again, and I would have to feel among ivy and honeysuckle for the stones and the sharp edge of the buried barrel. The hottest summer sun failed to reach this place. Privet hedge on one side had grown thick and tall as the caves of the house. There were trees and shrubs-which-had-turned-to-trees crowded on the other side.

On nearly every visit I had to twist off vines or bite them free with my teeth until I could locate the top of the pond, then pull up those lilies turning brown or which I thought had lived long enough. Very rarely one of them would bloom and float on the dark water like a boat which had been carved out of a white star. This one and surviving lilies for which I still had blooming hopes would be held back while with the edge of one hand I skimmed off the green scum and wiped it onto the grass. I can close my eyes now and be there again—leaves making a dapple of black shade and gray shade across my wrists. My fingers remember how the stem of the lily gives and pops off underwater;

it comes up slow and brown and slimy. I can still feel the ridge that top stave of the sunken barrel left on one palm and the patch of slicky scum on the other. All that—and yet I cannot remember hearing the song of a single bird.

Not until the day waned and it grew too dark to see was I called indoors and fed and, if my parents were expected late, put straightaway to bed on a fat feather mattress in Miss Carrie's room.

Sleep was not possible in that room, because of the wall curtains which lined it, and menaced and moved on all sides. It was like being Jack in Beanstalk Land, hidden in the folds of the giant's kimono.

Suspended from the top molding a foot below the ceiling, there was a high wooden shelf around all four walls, even across the windows. On the edge of that shelf old bedspreads of varying colors and patterns had been tacked like tent hangings. These reached from the molding to the floor. Miss Carrie's clothes, and Heaven knows *what* else, were stored behind these curtains, which billowed and swung so you could never predict where the next suspicious ripple would occur, or what unseen Thing set all that cloth in motion.

And on top of that high shelf just under the ceiling stood a thousand boxes—hat boxes, greeting-card boxes, corrugated boxes, suitcases, and one fine row of baskets. Could they have been sewing baskets? There were perhaps thirty of these in all shapes and colors and, like the mandolin, they were never to be touched. I wanted to feel their surfaces, terribly, but there was no way to reach that high shelf even with a broom handle. Miss Carrie had grown too old to go up the ladder and sometimes Granville would help her get something down, she said. Some baskets were woven in a round shape; one was an octagon with an amber handle; and the one I especially remember—brown and yellow—was formed in the shape of a castle-house, and little roofed towers lifted up on compartments while one entire golden wing was hinged to open out in another direction. I lay there wondering what was inside that row of baskets.

Struck wide-eyed and sleepless within four walls which breathed in the slightest air, sunk helplessly in the quicksand of that unfamiliar featherbed, I would lie tensely in the growing dark. Under my stare the baskets grew dimmer and dimmer and less believable. Sometimes they began to float before my mother's voice was heard in that house.

At the sound of her words and Miss Carrie answering, I always dropped instantly into relieved sleep. When next I came groggily awake Miss Carrie would be saying how good I had been and Mother, smiling, would whisper softly above the pillow that the sleep of the innocent was a wonderful thing.

Ingram Street was four city blocks of neat brick homes, except for Miss Carrie's. Her house was old-fashioned, had once been painted yellow, and was peeling. In front of the brick houses grew thin borders of thrift and candytuft and bulbs and spreading juniper. At Miss Carrie's the privet was shading her neighbors' flowers, and she tied a cow in the yard to crop the grass. The neighbors owned Scottie terriers and Siamese cats. Miss Carrie kept scrawny chickens who didn't mind plopping manure on sidewalks, or flapping to the edge of garbage cans to see what inside was still edible. Walking the three blocks to Miss Carrie's was like a stroll through the twentieth century; then, like a hole in time, you stepped down fifty years right at Miss Carrie's yard, and at the next house you could step back up into urban life. Daddy said half the city regulations on cows and indoor plumbing were finally started by Miss Carrie's neighbors, which may explain why she disliked them so much.

Next to her neighbor's brick garage was her rickety woodshed where pine slabs were stored for the kitchen stove. Another small building held kindling and corncobs, and beyond them both was her outhouse.

It was hard on Granville to live with an old aunt who still used an outdoor toilet. The summer between his junior and senior college years, he worked in the cotton gin to pay for plumbing, only to have Miss Carrie use that money for his tuition in the fall. He never brought any of his university friends home with him, or later his business friends, fearing they might need to go to the bathroom while they were there. ("So let them go!" cried Miss Carrie. "Damned if I will," said Granville.) Worse, he would never bring home prospective sweethearts to be inspected for the same reason. ("Your schooling has ruint you in more ways than one!" she complained. "What's *your* excuse?" he parried.)

The only time I ever heard Granville offer an argument that didn't fit the case had something to do with the outhouse. They had been fighting over flesh and spirit. He told her about brains and neurons and how Pavlov trained dogs. She started out with the soul, and said from the book of Job, "There is a spirit in man." At this he gave a sudden yell that if Aunt Carrie *really* believed man had a soul she would put a bathroom in that house. The whole thing upset Miss Carrie "pretty bad," she told my mother. It took them an hour to talk it over.

Besides the outhouse and those other buildings there were: fences, barn and barnyard, vegetable garden, stable, watering trough, twelve hens, an unpopular stray cat who bit the Siamese and—from time to time—kittens with odd colors in their fur. Miss Carrie's house was not unlike my buried pond; if you didn't know what was there you might trip at the edge of her yard and fall into an unexpected rural world.

It was the wrong world for Granville, who had been in a library he said was the size of the town hotel. But it was right for Miss Carrie. Even the skinny chickens and the cat with one tattered ear seemed tailored to match her bent form and her snuff-smeared chin.

For Miss Carrie was ugly. I wasn't allowed to say this, but any eyeball could tell it. Her hair, which had once been red, was now red and brown and gray mixed, wadded behind in a stingy knot that wouldn't hold it all. Always her neck was full of the mottled stuff.

In her youth, too, Miss Carrie had been freckled. Now her face had fallen in wrinkles so that freckles and liver spots were trapped inside the folds. A shift of her face and some new blemish sprang suddenly into view while another slipped out of sight.

She was a small woman, not much bigger than I, and rheumatism had twisted her a little to one side. Grim glasses with steel edges rested on the tip of her nose, where they wouldn't inconvenience her vision. The color of her eyes was the color of worn mahogany; sometimes I thought the wet snuff had permeated them. And her walk was rapid, half scrabbling to incorporate that lopsided lurch into her gait. Miss Carrie was ugly, and the first time I saw her I maybe was afraid. I can't remember the first time.

Yet I loved Miss Carrie. She refused to play games. She would not converse except on matters which interested her and bewildered me. She seldom gave presents, and then they were the sort of thing a child dislikes—one breadplate ringed around in gold script, "Give us this day our daily bread," which I was to save against the day of my marriage. She did not even believe that I would grow up to be an artist and never marry. When I spun out my future in a shining web her thoughts were on milking time.

What did I love in her then?

Her love for me.

Because I *pleased* her—though she never said so. She did not hear a single important word I spoke, but she did listen to the general sound of me. Discolored by snuff and spit, her grin was approving. She allowed me to water her potted plants with that cream pitcher which was a hundred years old; nobody had ever trusted me that much before, and not a whole lot have since.

I never thought twice about her loving me, about deserving it or returning it or being especially obedient because of it. Love was simply mixed into those days the way that biscuit odor lay in the rooms of the house. You forgot to notice. Nostril and heart, having once put the thing on record, moved on to something else.

Some days I was with Miss Carrie for milking time, and through the barnyard we went together, I a stealthy mimic coming behind her, playing at being old, playing at being ugly—neither of which I ever thought possible for me to be.

Inside the stall, Miss Carrie would halfway crumple under the cow. It was the only way she could manage, folding down first and easing up again to the level of the stool. Her dress tail dragged in manure. It was embarrassing. I didn't feel like imitating that.

In the house again with a pail of warm milk, we waited for Granville. Since he had earned his degree from Chapel Hill and nailed it over that roll-top desk in the front room, he ran an insurance office and turned his money over to Miss Carrie, who kept feeding it to banks.

("People sell insurance that never go to college," my mother said. "I can't see it helped him much."

"He ain't working in a cotton mill like me," growled my daddy.)

"Aunt Carrie?"

We heard the front door bang and his steps, as even as a march, came down the hall.

"Back porch!" she'd scream. Even when Miss Carrie smiled her voice was sharp and loud and kept a whine in it. Thinking back, I suppose she talked through her nose. All I heard then was the ugliness, another example of how I would never sound.

Granville patted her on the back—I never saw them kiss—and crowed something crazy at me and lifted me onto his shoulders where I could enjoy his beautiful hair. Granville's black hair was curly, almost kinky. Thrust one finger into it and a strand twined up like living ivy.

("Makes you wonder about that family tree," my mother said. "His papa *did* leave her, and they gave Miss Carrie the boy."

"I reckon you think that would explain everything." answered my daddy.)

Granville chuckled when I pushed all my fingers into his hair. My hands were tied to his scalp with wire. "Punkin, what you been into today?" Granville took nibbles from my kneecaps. I clamped them tight to choke him and he bent forward as if to throw me over.

"Don't hurt her!" said Miss Carrie. "Granville, I'm leaving cold supper in the safe for you two so I can get to prayer meeting. Her mama's coming about seven-thirty."

My knees could feel vibrations in his throat. Granville was grinding his teeth. It angered him that Miss Carrie would struggle like a grasshopper the five blocks to the church, people out in the cool of the evening watching her pass, feeling sorry for her. Granville thought she blamed him for the lack of a car the way he blamed her for the outhouse.

"You could miss prayer meeting one Wednesday night," he complained. "Something good on the radio tonight."

She put her apron away and went to her bedroom, to get something from behind those throbbing walls or out of the castle basket.

We were eating on the oilcloth in the kitchen when Miss Carrie came out, unchanged except for a black straw hat with spindly bunches of lilac around the crown, her dress tail still damp where she had scrubbed briefly at stains from the barn. Maybe she had rinsed her mouth of snuff. No more.

She said politely, "Now you come back, honey. Tell your mama I enjoyed having you." She said, "Guess you don't want to come along, Granville?"

Then we could hear the sound of her sensible shoes, hitting out of rhythm, *hard*-soft, *hard*-soft, down the hall, past that doorway showing the crutch and the mandolin, past the geraniums and ferns. Gone.

Granville pushed food into an angry face. I intended to be tactful and not talk but there was so much to tell him—a movie where hands came out of a bedroom wall where a beautiful girl was sleeping, dirt daubers under the front steps; and this scratch, right here on the arm—would I get lockjaw?

Interesting, he said. Fine, he said. No.

Absently he mangled the last biscuit in his fingers. Then he looked down at the plate of cold crumbs and said one of those swear words they had taught him at Chapel Hill.

I was glad when Mama came.

My daddy liked Granville. He would not side with Granville against my mother and Miss Carrie, but sometimes he would wink or hold his thumb up or down in the air beyond their view. Five years back he had spent two days at the university as Granville's guest. My daddy had started working in the textile mill before he ever finished high school; he couldn't get over that place in Chapel Hill—all that land and those big buildings. And not a factory, not a place where you could hold some finished product in your hand. There was no way to tell whether a college was failing or succeeding, my daddy said. It must be happening around you on all sides, success or failure; but it would be years before anybody knew which.

I can imagine his telling this to Granville and Granville saying, "You mean the utilitarian aspects are long range," and Daddy scowling, "That's what I said, ain't it?"

From that one visit to the state university, Daddy brought home a stack of small picture cards of campus scenes, each not much bigger than a postage stamp, and stacked in a tiny wooden box. Later he gave the set to me. On rainy days we shuffled through the library, the administration building, the old well, the stadium, the science lab. He showed which buildings he had gone inside with Granville.

"Someday you might go to college," he'd say wistfully. "When my ship comes in."

During the August I was eight years old Mama spent a day with her sick sister, so my daddy walked with me to Miss Carrie's, where I was to stay till his shift was over at the mill. I didn't much want to go.

"You're mighty quiet."

I said I was counting how many steps it took to get from our house to Miss Carrie's. That was true, but mostly I didn't want my feet to take those steps at all. I wanted Miss Carrie and Granville to be right about everything from prayer meeting on up and down. If they couldn't both be right, I'd rather stay home than sit by that pond and wonder which was more right than the other.

Daddy looked at me hard but he didn't speak again till we were nearly there. "Watch for a surprise today," he said. He sounded nervous.

"Something from Mama?"

He was hasty in eliminating hope of any gift when she came home from her sister's. "Nothing like that. Something new at Miss Carrie's. Something you won't expect to see."

I couldn't imagine. Miss Carrie never bought anything. Even the hat with the lilacs was an old one of my mother's. Granville had built the radio out of three used sets he got for nothing.

I thought Miss Carrie might have proved she owned a soul by installing the indoor plumbing at last. Since I preferred the outhouse and the thrill of wondering if the granddaddy longlegs would make his stilting march across my bare toes, I didn't much favor that bathroom. But I did want the arguments to end. If Miss Carrie had put in a toilet, I would have to start brushing my teeth at her house.

Miss Carrie was waiting, as usual, on her porch, fanning with the *Sunday School Journal*. As Mama's substitute, my daddy went through a feeble form of the talk ritual. I had my glass of milk with cornbread crumbled into it. Then I went outdoors, enjoying the mock resignation of the task of cleaning the pond again.

I stopped so suddenly one foot hung in the air and I nearly fell. This time the undergrowth had been chopped back and there were branches and lengths of vine turning brown in piles around the yard. Dead leaves had been raked away. The water in the pond had been opened up to the sky like a mouth, and although it was still dirty a nearby hose hinted that fresh water had been added—an improvement I had never thought of making and now resented. I began to quiver from rage. Which of them . . . which of them had dared . . . Was it Granville or Miss Carrie who, after years of neglect, now came tramping into my place and stole my work and—by making it neat at last—killed all the joy forever?

I grabbed a rock to throw and shatter what they had done, and then something flashed. A mirror moved inside the pond, or else light was shining all the way up from China through a chink in that inverted floor. I lowered the rock and got on all fours. My nose nearly touched the water. Suddenly the surface folded up once on itself and a bubble came to the top and paused and broke; and I saw the goldfish.

He was black and orange, a parody of a tiger. He flicked away under a lily pad and waited, then darted across to another.

I saw then a box left conveniently near the pond full of crumbs and oatmeal, and I scattered these with a gesture of spread fingers, the way God must have thrown forth a solar system onto the night.

The long August afternoon I hovered over the pond till my knees ached, watching that elusive fish, sometimes losing him in shadow and having him found again by a glint of sunlight. He would arch upward to gobble and dive again, swimming at the food in a pattern of arrowheads. Large bread chunks he dragged underneath to separate; others he gulped whole. He seemed to vanish and reappear, like a light going on, going off. Here, gone. There, gone.

Once and for all I wanted to prove whether eyes located on each side of the tiny head could really see me dead ahead, and I kept wagging my body trying to stand in the very center. Each time I froze in the proper place he disappeared and took the perspective with him. Once he brushed ever so lightly against my dangling thumb and I drew it out in wonder and held it, wet and still tingling, in the warm place underneath my chin.

The times I could see him I gave myself over to the delight of seeing him, but when he dived into the dark I worried. Whose handiwork was the goldfish? I tried to touch his fin and he thrust himself to the depths. Who had surprised me with this splendid lighted thing?

It was Granville, of course. It was typical of Granville, his pockets heavy with chewing gum, his head of hair growing into a private game. Once he had taken me to the circus and paid for everything. It had to be Granville who had cleaned the pond and hid the golden fish for me.

The fish shot to the top and rode across it almost like a boat, slicing the water with a transparent tail. I reached for him and he swam to China.

No, no, it had to be Miss Carrie who had fixed the pond. She was the one who knew about it, had once kept minnows there. She had described the dangers of drowning, while Granville had never said a word. And wasn't it Miss Carrie who liked animals—her cow, those chickens, the scarred cat?

Now that I thought about it, she had even hinted. With my own ears, just as we came up the walk that day, I had heard her tell Daddy she was fanning with the *Sunday School Journal*, having just read the lesson on "fishers of men." There! Wasn't that a clue? Wasn't she telling me then?

No, it had to be Granville. He loved surprises. At the circus he once bought six boxes of Cracker Jack just to get the little toys. So it had to be Granville, even if he didn't own a car to drive Miss Carrie to prayer meeting. Yet wasn't it bound to be Miss Carrie who had given this gleaming fish, even if she wouldn't put a bathroom in the house?

I knew it was one of them but not both who had put this brightness in my pool. And I couldn't choose. I wanted it to be both. If Granville had only cleared the underbrush . . . if Miss Carrie had only slipped the fish into the water . . .

I did not believe it had been both of them together, yet it had to be nothing less.

Not until they called me twice would I go indoors. I said nothing about that fish wearing its colors of Halloween. Eating in silence I would not mention the underbrush cleared or the water made pure in my pool, or the long afternoon I had spent trying to catch on my fingers that flying piece of light beneath the surface.

Behind the tumbler of milk I watched them. I waited for one to say, "How did you like my fish?" I waited for one to confess and one to be silent.

Both Granville and Miss Carrie looked tickled and secretive. The one who had given the fish had clearly told the other; but which was which? *Oh, let it be both!* I thought, but I knew it was not.

We finished the apple dumpling. Miss Carrie cleared the table. She and Granville had begun to look bewildered, worried, at last a little hurt. Eyebrows were raised over my head and shoulders were shrugged. Still I would say nothing. I kept the fish inside me where it burned and shone, but I never looked directly into the face of Granville or Miss Carrie for fear of dividing them one from the other, forever.

At last my daddy came to take me home. He could tell something was wrong.

Usually I liked to walk home after dark and see how things changed when the light went out of the world, but tonight I hurried. He asked, "What was the surprise?"

I answered that they—yes, I said *they*—had cleaned out the pond. That's all I told him. Once he glanced back toward the lighted windows. Were the lights shining in Miss Carrie's room or in Granville's? I wouldn't turn my head. We walked home without much conversation.

When next I went to Miss Carrie's I couldn't find the goldfish anywhere, and although the vines were growing back over the water none of my fingers cared any more. I didn't even play there, and I didn't ask a word about the fish. I guess it died.

The Patented Gate and the Mean Hamburger

Robert Penn Warren

YOU have seen him a thousand times. You have seen him standing on the street corner on Saturday afternoon, in the little county-seat towns. He wears blue jean pants, or overalls washed to a pale pastel blue like the color of sky after a shower in spring, but because it is Saturday he has on a wool coat, an old one, perhaps the coat left from the suit he got married in a long time back. His long wrist bones hang out from the sleeves of the coat, the tendons showing along the bone like the dry twist of grapevine still corded on the stovelength of a hickory sapling you would find in his wood box beside his cookstove among the split chunks of gum and red oak. The big hands, with the knotted, cracked joints and the square, horn-thick nails, hang loose off the wrist bone like clumsy, home-made tools hung on the wall of a shed after work. If it is summer, he wears a straw hat with a wide brim, the straw fraying loose around the edge. If it is winter, he wears a felt hat, black once, but now weathered with streaks of dark gray and dull purple in the sunlight. His face is long and bony, the jawbone long under the drawn-in cheeks. The flesh along the jawbone is nicked in a couple of places where the unaccustomed razor has been drawn over the leathercoarse skin. A tiny bit of blood crusts brown where the nick is. The color of the face is red, a dull red like the red clay mud or clay dust which clings to the bottom of his pants and to the cast-iron-looking brogans on his feet, or a red like the color of a piece of hewed cedar which has been left in the weather. The face does not look alive. It seems to be molded from the clay or hewed from the cedar. When the jaw moves, once, with its deliberate, massive motion on the quid of tobacco, you are still not convinced. That motion is but the cunning triumph of a mechanism concealed within.

But you see the eyes. You see that the eyes are alive. They are pale blue or gray, set back under the deep brows and thorny eyebrows. They are not wide, but are squinched up like eyes accustomed to wind or sun or to measuring the stroke of the ax or to fixing the object over the rifle sights. When you pass, you see that the eyes are alive and are warily and dispassionately estimating you from the ambush of the thorny brows. Then you pass on, and he stands there in that stillness which is his gift.

With him may be standing two or three others like himself, but they are still, too. They do not talk. The young men, who will be like these men when they get to be fifty or sixty, are down at the beer parlor, carousing and laughing with a high, whickering laugh. But the men on the corner are long past all that. They are past many things. They have endured and will endure in their silence and wisdom. They will stand on the street corner and reject the world which passes under their level gaze as a rabble passes under the guns of a rocky citadel around whose base a slatternly town has assembled.

I had seen Jeff York a thousand times, or near, standing like that on the street corner in town, while the people flowed past him, under the distant and wary and dispassionate eyes in ambush. He would be waiting for his wife and the three towheaded children who were walking around the town looking into store windows and at the people. After a while they would come back to him, and then, wordlessly, he would lead them to the store where they always did their trading. He would go first, marching with a steady bent-kneed stride, setting the cast-iron brogans down deliberately on the cement; then his wife, a small woman with covert, sidewise, curious glances for the world, would follow, and behind her the towheads bunched together in a dazed, glory-struck way. In the store, when their turn came, Jeff York would move to the counter, accept the clerk's greeting, and then bend down from his height to catch the whispered directions of his wife. He would straighten up and say, "Gimme a sack of flahr, if'n you please." Then when the sack of flour had been brought, he would lean again to his wife for the next item. When the stuff had all been bought and paid for with the grease-thick, wadded dollar bills which he took from an old leather coin purse with a metal catch to it, he would heave it all together into his arms and march out, his wife and towheads behind him and his eyes fixed level over the heads of the crowd. He would march down the street and around to the hitching lot where the wagons were, and put his stuff into his wagon and cover it with an old quilt to wait till he got ready to drive out to his place.

For Jeff York had a place. That was what made him different from the other men who looked like him and with whom he stood on the street corner on Saturday afternoon. They were croppers, but he, Jeff York, had a place. But he stood with them because his father had stood with their fathers and his grandfathers with their grandfathers, or with men like their fathers and grandfathers, in other towns, in settlements in the mountains, in towns beyond the mountains. They were the great-great-great-grandsons of men who, half woodsmen and half farmers, had been shoved into the sand hills, into the limestone hills, into the barrens, two hundred, two hundred and fifty years before and had learned there the way to grabble a life out of the sand and the stone. And when the soil had leached away into the sand or burnt off the stone, they went on west, walking with the bent-kneed stride over the mountains, their eyes squinching warily in the gaunt faces, the rifle over the crooked arm, hunting a new place.

But there was a curse on them. They only knew the life they knew, and that life did not belong to the fat bottom lands, where the cane was head-tall, and to the grassy meadows and the rich swale. So they passed those places by and hunted for the place which was like home and where they could pick up the old life, with the same feel in the bones and the squirrel's bark sounding the same after first light. They had walked a long way, to the sand hills of Alabama, to the red country of North Mississippi and Louisiana, to the Barrens of Tennessee, to the Knobs of Kentucky and the scrub country of West Kentucky, to the Ozarks. Some of them had stopped in Cobb County, Tennessee, in the hilly eastern part of the county, and had built their cabins and dug up the ground for the corn patch. But the land had washed away there, too, and in the end they had come down out of the high land into the bottoms—for half of Cobb County is a rich, swelling country—where the corn was good and the tobacco unfurled a leaf like a yard of green velvet and the white houses stood among the cedars and tulip trees and maples. But they were not to live in the white houses with the limestone chimneys set strong at the end of each gable. No, they were to live in the shacks on the back of the farms, or in cabins not much different from the cabins they had once lived in two hundred years before over the mountains or, later, in the hills of Cobb County. But the shacks and the cabins now stood on somebody else's ground, and the curse which they had brought with them over the mountain trail, more precious than the bullet mold or grandma's quilt, the curse which was the very feeling in the bones and the habit in the hand, had come full circle.

Jeff York was one of those men, but he had broken the curse.

It had taken him more than thirty years to do it, from the time when he was nothing but a big boy until he was fifty. It had taken him from sun to sun, year in and year out, and all the sweat in his body, and all the power of rejection he could muster, until the very act of rejection had become a kind of pleasure, a dark, secret, savage dissipation, like an obsessing vice. But those years had given him his place, sixty acres with a house and barn.

When he bought the place, it was not very good. The land was run-down from years of neglect and abuse. But Jeff York put brush in the gullies to stop the wash and planted clover on the run-down fields. He mended the fences, rod by rod. He patched the roof on the little house and propped up the porch, buying the lumber and shingles almost piece by piece and one by one as he could spare the sweat-bright and grease-slick quarters and half-dollars out of his leather purse. Then he painted the house. He painted it white, for he knew that that was the color you painted a house sitting back from the road with its couple of maples, beyond the clover field.

Last, he put up the gate. It was a patented gate, the kind you can ride up to and open by pulling on a pull rope without getting off your horse or out of your buggy or wagon. It had a high pair of posts, well braced and with a high crossbar between, and the bars for the opening mechanism extending on each side. It was painted white, too. Jeff was even prouder of the gate than he was of the place. Lewis Simmons, who lived next to Jeff's place, swore he had seen Jeff come out after dark on a mule and ride in and out of that gate, back and forth, just for the pleasure of pulling on the rope and making the mechanism work. The gate was the seal Jeff York had put on all the years of sweat and rejection. He could sit on his porch on a Sunday afternoon in summer, before milking time, and look down the rise, down the winding dirt track, to the white gate beyond the clover, and know what he needed to know about all the years passed.

Meanwhile Jeff York had married and had had the three towheads. His wife was twenty years or so younger than he, a small, dark woman, who walked with her head bowed a little and from that humble and unprovoking posture stole sidewise, secret glances at the world from eyes which were brown or black—you never could tell which because you never remembered having looked her straight in the eye—and which were surprisingly bright in that sidewise, secret flicker, like the eyes of a small, cunning bird which surprise you from the brush. When they came to town she moved along the street, with a child in her arms or later with the three trailing behind her, and stole her looks at the world. She wore a calico dress, dun-colored, which hung loose to conceal whatever shape her thin body had, and in winter over the dress a brown wool coat with a scrap of fur at the collar which looked like some tattered growth of fungus feeding on old wood. She wore black high-heeled shoes, slippers of some kind, which she kept polished and which surprised you under that dress and coat. In the slippers she moved with a slightly limping, stealthy gait, almost sliding them along the pavement, as though she had not fully mastered the complicated trick required to use them properly. You knew that she wore them only when she came to town, that she carried them wrapped up in a piece of newspaper until their wagon had reached the first house on the outskirts of town, and that, on the way back, at the same point, she would take them off and wrap them up again and hold the bundle in her lap until she got home. If the weather happened to be bad, or if it was winter, she would have a pair of old brogans under the wagon seat.

It was not that Jeff York was a hard man and kept his wife in clothes that were as bad as those worn by the poorest of the women of the croppers. In fact, some of the cropper women, poor or not, black or white, managed to buy dresses with some color in them and proper hats, and went to the moving picture show on Saturday afternoon. But Jeff still owed a little money on his place, less than two hundred dollars, which he had had to borrow to rebuild his barn after it was struck by lightning. He had, in fact, never been entirely out of debt. He had lost a mule which had got out on the highway and been hit by a truck. That had set him back. One of his towheads had been sickly for a couple of winters. He had not been in deep, but he was not a man, with all those years of rejection behind him, to forget the meaning of those years. He was good enough to his family. Nobody ever said the contrary. But he was good to them in terms of all the years he had lived through. He did what he could afford. He bought the towheads a ten-cent bag of colored candy every Saturday afternoon for them to suck on during the ride home in the wagon, and the last thing before they left town, he always took the lot of them over to the dogwagon to get hamburgers and orange pop.

The towheads were crazy about hamburgers. And so was his wife, for that matter. You could tell it, even if she didn't say anything, for she would lift her bowed-forward head a little, and her face would brighten, and she would run her tongue out to wet her lips just as the plate with the hamburger would be set on the counter before her. But all those folks, like Jeff York and his family, like hamburgers, with pickle and onions and mustard and tomato catsup, the whole works. It is something different. They stay out in the country and eat hog-meat, when they can get it, and greens and corn bread and potatoes, and nothing but a pinch of salt to brighten it on the tongue, and when they get to town and get hold of beef and wheat bread and all the stuff to jack up the flavor, they have to swallow to keep the mouth from flooding before they even take the first bite.

So the last thing every Saturday, Jeff York would take his family over to Slick Hardin's *Dew Drop Inn Diner* and give them the treat. The diner was built like a railway coach, but it was set on a concrete foundation on a lot just off the main street of town. At each end the concrete was painted to show wheels. Slick Hardin kept the grass just in front of the place pretty well mowed and one or two summers he even had a couple of flower beds in the middle of that shirttail-size lawn. Slick had a good business. For a few years he had been a prelim fighter over in Nashville and had got his name in the papers a few times. So he was a kind of hero, with the air of romance about him. He had been born, however, right in town and, as soon as he had found out he wasn't ever going to be good enough to be a real fighter, he had come back home and started the dogwagon, the first one ever in town. He was a slick-skinned fellow, about thirty-five, prematurely bald, with his head slick all over. He had big eyes, pale blue and slick looking like agates. When he said something that he thought smart, he would roll his eyes around, slick in his head like marbles, to see who was laughing. Then he'd wink. He had done very well with his business, for despite the fact that he had picked up city ways and a lot of city talk, he still remembered enough to deal with the country people, and they were the ones who brought the dimes in. People who lived right there in town, except for school kids in the afternoon and the young toughs from the pool room or men on the night shift down at the railroad, didn't often get around to the dogwagon.

Slick Hardin was perhaps trying to be smart when he said what he did to Mrs. York. Perhaps he had forgotten, just for that moment, that people like Jeff York and his wife didn't like to be kidded, at least not in that way. He said what he did, and then grinned and rolled his eyes around to see if some of the other people present were thinking it was funny.

Mrs. York was sitting on a stool in front of the counter, flanked on one side by Jeff York and on the other by the three towheads. She had just sat down to wait for the hamburger—there were several orders in ahead of the York order—and had been watching in her sidewise fashion every move of Slick Hardin's hands as he patted the pink meat onto the hot slab and wiped the split buns over the greasy iron to make them ready to receive it. She always watched him like that, and when the hamburger was set before her she would wet her lips with her tongue.

That day Slick set the hamburger down in front of Mrs. York, and said, "Anybody likes hamburger much as you, Mrs. York, ought to git him a hamburger stand."

Mrs. York flushed up, and didn't say anything, staring at her plate. Slick rolled his eyes to see how it was going over, and somebody down the counter snickered. Slick looked back at the Yorks, and if he had not been so encouraged by the snicker he might, when he saw Jeff York's face, have hesitated before going on with his kidding. People like Jeff York are touchous, and they are especially touchous about the womenfolks, and you do not make jokes with or about their womenfolks unless it is perfectly plain that the joke is a very special kind of friendly joke. The snicker down the counter had defined the joke as not entirely friendly. Jeff was looking at Slick, and something was growing slowly in that hewed-cedar face, and back in the gray eyes in the ambush of thorny brows.

But Slick did not notice. The snicker had encouraged him, and so he said, "Yeah, if I liked them hamburgers much as you, I'd buy me a hamburger stand. Fact, I'm selling this one. You want to buy it?"

There was another snicker, louder, and Jeff York, whose hamburger had been about half way to his mouth for another bite, laid it down deliberately on his plate. But whatever might have happened at that moment did not happen. It did not happen because Mrs. York lifted her flushed face, looked straight at Slick Hardin, swallowed hard to get down a piece of the hamburger or to master her nerve, and said in a sharp, strained voice, "You sellen this place?"

There was complete silence. Nobody had expected her to say anything. The chances were she had never said a word in that diner in the couple of hundred times she had been in it. She had come in with Jeff York and, when a stool had come vacant, had sat down, and Jeff had said, "Gimme five hamburgers, if'n you please, and make 'em well done, and five bottles of orange pop." Then, after the eating was over, he had always laid down seventy-five cents on the counter—that is, after there were five hamburger-eaters in the family—and walked out, putting his brogans down slow, and his wife and kids following without a word. But now she spoke up and asked the question, in that strained, artificial voice, and everybody, including her husband, looked at her with surprise.

As soon as he could take it in, Slick Hardin replied, "Yeah, I'm selling it."

She swallowed hard again, but this time it could not have been hamburger, and demanded, "What you asken fer hit?"

Slick looked at her in the new silence, half shrugged, a little contemptuously, and said, "Fourteen hundred and fifty dollars."

She looked back at him, while the blood ebbed from her face. "Hit's a lot of money," she said in a flat tone, and returned her gaze to the hamburger on her plate.

"Lady," Slick said defensively, "I got that much money tied up here. Look at that there stove. It is a *Heat Master* and they cost. Them coffee urns, now. Money can't buy no better. And this here lot, lady, the diner sets on. Anybody knows I got that much money tied up here. I got more. This lot cost me more'n . . ." He suddenly realized that she was not listening to him. And he must have realized, too, that she didn't have a dime in the world and couldn't buy his diner, and that he was making a fool of himself, defending his price. He stopped abruptly, shrugged his shoulders, and then swung his wide gaze down the counter to pick out somebody to wink to.

But before he got the wink off, Jeff York had said, "Mr. Hardin."

Slick looked at him and asked, "Yeah?"

"She didn't mean no harm," Jeff York said. "She didn't mean to be messen in yore business."

Slick shrugged. "Ain't no skin off my nose," he said. "Ain't no secret I'm selling out. My price ain't no secret neither."

Mrs. York bowed her head over her plate. She was chewing a mouthful of her hamburger with a slow, abstracted motion of her jaw, and you knew that it was flavorless on her tongue.

That was, of course, on a Saturday. On Thursday afternoon of the next week Slick was in the diner alone. It was the slack time, right in the middle of the afternoon. Slick, as he told it later, was wiping off the stove and wasn't noticing. He was sort of whistling to himself, he said. He had a way of whistling soft through his teeth. But he wasn't whistling loud, he said, not so loud he wouldn't have heard the door open or the steps if she hadn't come gum-shoeing in on him to stand there waiting in the middle of the floor until he turned round and was so surprised he nearly had heart failure. He had thought he was there alone, and there she was, watching every move he was making, like a cat watching a goldfish swim in a bowl.

"Howdy-do," he said, when he got his breath back.

"This place still fer sale?" she asked him.

"Yeah, lady," he said.

"What you asken fer hit?"

"Lady, I done told you," Slick replied, "fourteen hundred and fifty dollars."

"Hit's a heap of money," she said.

Slick started to tell her how much money he had tied up there, but before he had got going, she had turned and slipped out of the door.

"Yeah," Slick said later to the men who came into the diner, "me like a fool starting to tell her how much money I got tied up here when I knowed she didn't have a dime. That woman's crazy. She must walked that five or six miles in here just to ask me something she already knowed the answer to. And then turned right round and walked out. But I am selling me this place. I'm tired of slinging hash to them hicks. I got me some connections over in Nashville and I'm gonna open me a place over there. A cigar stand and about three pool tables and maybe some beer. I'll have me a sort of club in the back. You know, membership cards to git in, where the boys will play a little game. Just sociable. I got good connections over in Nashville. I'm selling this place. But that woman, she ain't got a dime. She ain't gonna buy it."

But she did.

On Saturday Jeff York led his family over to the diner. They ate hamburgers without a word and marched out. After they had gone, Slick said, "Looks like she ain't going to make the invest-mint. Gonna buy a block of bank stock instead." Then he rolled his eyes, located a brother down the counter, and winked.

It was almost the end of the next week before it happened. What had been going on inside the white house out on Jeff York's place nobody knew or was to know. Perhaps she just starved him out, just not doing the cooking or burning everything. Perhaps she just quit attending to the children properly and he had to come back tired from work and take care of them. Perhaps she just lay in bed at night and talked and talked to him, asking him to buy it, nagging him all night long, while he would fall asleep and then wake up with a start to hear her voice still going on. Or perhaps she just turned her face away from him and wouldn't let him touch her. He was a lot older than she, and she was probably the only woman he had ever had. He had been too ridden by his dream and his passion for rejection during all the years before to lay even a finger on a woman. So she had him there. Because he was a lot older and because he had never had another woman. But perhaps she used none of these methods. She was a small, dark, cunning woman, with a sidewise look from her lowered face, and she could have thought up ways of her own, no doubt.

Whatever she thought up, it worked. On Friday morning Jeff York went to the bank. He wanted to mortgage his place, he told Todd Sullivan, the president. He wanted fourteen hundred and fifty dollars, he said. Todd Sullivan would not let him have it. He already owed the bank one hundred and sixty dollars and the best he could get on a mortgage was eleven hundred dollars. That was in 1935 and then farmland wasn't worth much and half the land in the country was mortgaged anyway. Jeff York sat in the chair by Todd Sullivan's desk and didn't say anything. Eleven hundred dollars would not do him any good. Take off the hundred and sixty he owed and it wouldn't be but a little over nine hundred dollars clear to him. He sat there quietly for a minute, apparently turning that fact over in his head. Then Todd Sullivan asked him, "How much you say you need?"

Jeff York told him.

"What you want it for?" Todd Sullivan asked.

He told him that.

"I tell you," Todd Sullivan said, "I don't want to stand in the way of a man bettering himself. Never did. That diner ought to be a good proposition, all right, and I don't want to stand in your way if you want to come to town and better yourself. It will be a step up from that farm for you, and I like a man has got ambition. The bank can't lend you the money, not on that piece of property. But I tell you what I'll do. I'll buy your place. I got me some walking horses I'm keeping out on my father's place. But I could use me a little place of my own. For my horses. I'll give you seventeen hundred for it. Cash."

Jeff York did not say anything to that. He looked slow at Todd Sullivan as though he did not understand.

"Seventeen hundred," the banker repeated. "That's a good figure. For these times."

Jeff was not looking at him now. He was looking out the

window, across the alleyway—Todd Sullivan's office was in the back of the bank. The banker, telling about it later when the doings of Jeff York had become for a moment a matter of interest, said, "I thought he hadn't even heard me. He looked like he was half asleep or something. I coughed to sort of wake him up. You know the way you do. I didn't want to rush him. You can't rush those people, you know. But I couldn't sit there all day. I had offered him a fair price."

It was, as a matter of fact, a fair price for the times, when the bottom was out of everything in the section.

Jeff York took it. He took the seventeen hundred dollars and bought the dogwagon with it, and rented a little house on the edge of town and moved in with his wife and the towheads. The first day after they got settled, Jeff York and his wife went over to the diner to get instructions from Slick about running the place. He showed Mrs. York all about how to work the coffee machine and the stove, and how to make up the sandwiches, and how to clean the place up after herself. She fried up hamburgers for all of them, herself, her husband, and Slick Hardin, for practice, and they ate the hamburgers while a couple of hangers-on watched them. "Lady," Slick said, for he had money in his pocket and was heading out for Nashville on the seven o'clock train that night, and was feeling expansive, "lady, you sure fling a mean hamburger."

He wiped the last crumbs and mustard off his lips, got his valise from behind the door, and said, "Lady, git in there and pitch. I hope you make a million hamburgers." Then he stepped out into the bright fall sunshine and walked away whistling up the street, whistling through his teeth and rolling his eyes as though there were somebody to wink to. That was the last anybody in town ever saw of Slick Hardin.

The next day, Jeff York worked all day down at the diner. He was scrubbing up the place inside and cleaning up the trash which had accumulated behind it. He burned all the trash. Then he gave the place a good coat of paint outside, white paint. That took him two days. Then he touched up the counter inside with varnish. He straightened up the sign out front, which had begun to sag a little. He had that place looking spick and span.

Then on the fifth day after they got settled—it was Sunday—he took a walk in the country. It was along toward sun when he started out, not late, as a matter of fact, for by October the days are shortening up. He walked out the Curtisville pike and out the cut-off leading to his farm. When he entered the cut-off, about a mile from his own place, it was still light enough for the Bowdoins, who had a filling station at the corner, to see him plain when he passed.

The next time anybody saw him was on Monday morning about six o'clock. A man taking milk into town saw him. He was hanging from the main cross bar of the white patented gate. He had jumped off the gate. But he had propped the thing open so there wouldn't be any chance of clambering back up on it if his neck didn't break when he jumped and he should happen to change his mind.

But that was an unnecessary precaution, as it developed. Dr. Stauffer said that his neck was broken very clean. "A man who can break a neck as clean as that could make a living at it," Dr. Stauffer said. And added, "If he's damned sure it ain't ever his own neck."

Mrs. York was much cut up by her husband's death. People were sympathetic and helpful, and out of a mixture of sympathy and curiosity she got a good starting trade at the diner. And the trade kept right on. She got so she didn't hang her head and look sidewise at you and the world. She would look straight at you. She got so she could walk in high heels without giving the impression that it was a trick she was learning. She wasn't a bad-looking woman, as a matter of fact, once she had caught on how to fix herself up a little. The railroad men and the pool hall gang liked to hang out there and kid with her. Also, they said, she flung a mean hamburger.

The Elect

Peter Taylor

THOUGH it was past two in the afternoon, Judge Larwell was still sleeping like a baby. The best thing his wife could do was to keep busy. The telephone was off the hook, and the doorbell had been muffled. It was really as though someone were dead and black crepe were draped on the front door. Actually, their faithful son-in-law Joseph, along with several other of Judge Larwell's ardent supporters—and two state troopers, as well—was stationed on the wide front porch to receive and ultimately drive away any of the television people or even any of the party's own public-relations people who might come banging on the door. The judge had fought a long, hard battle, and he had won. He was now governor-elect of the state. Surely the governor-elect was entitled to his rest. In his wife's opinion, at any rate, among the spoils belonging to the victor there should be included at least some small measure of privacy.

When the wall clock in the downstairs hallway struck a quarter past two, the state's first lady-elect was at her desk at the end of the living room, writing checks. She was paying last month's bills from the department stores and the oil company, from the grocer and the dry cleaner and the drugstore. In the last weeks of the campaign, she had let everything go. As a matter of fact, she had actually taken up residence in a suite of rooms at the hotel opposite the capitol building. She had lived as she had never imagined she could possibly live. She had, in those last weeks, joined in the campaign and, much as she hated it all, had taken to the road with the rest of the family, appearing on platforms in twenty counties, waving, smiling, giving the victory sign.

She had even made half a dozen impromptu two-minute speeches when nobody else from the judge's family was there to speak up. Even the opposition newspapers had called her a good trouper and had said she was "well-spoken." Her best and most oft-quoted words were those delivered to a jokester in a crowd, who had called out, asking if she wanted to go keep house in that "musty old governor's mansion." She had replied with: "Whither he goes, there I shall go also. His people shall be my people." And the crowd had roared its crude, infelicitous approval: "Give 'em hell, Nell."

But now it was over. In the hotel ballroom at 3 a.m., posturing before the television cameras, Judge Larwell's opposition had conceded. The race was over. And now the judge's wife could once again enjoy the dignity of being Mrs. Larwell and not Nell Larwell, as the newspapers—opposition and otherwise—had insisted on calling her. During the campaign, you had to endure almost anything—that is, you did if, in the modern way, you joined in the fray alongside your husband.

Halfway through the campaign, when things began to seem uncertain for the judge and she had to begin climbing on platforms and making a spectacle of herself, she realized who were the two most sympathetic figures in American public life. They were Bess Truman and Mamie Eisenhower. Clearly, those two had hated it all as much as she had. They were women of "some background," like herself. And like herself, they had recognized their duty and had carried on. Everyone had said that she, unlike them, must have known what to expect, coming as she did from a political family—having even once, as a child, lived in the "musty old mansion."

But in her papa's day, it had been different. In those days, a candidate's wife stayed at home with her family, went her usual social rounds, got her bills paid on time. The intrusions of television and the pressures from PR men had not existed then. It had been very different. Mrs. Larwell's mother, as first lady of the state, had said that the principal adjustment she had had to make was to the ever-present sense of living beyond her means. Yes, in those days the family of a successful politician had to learn to live like rich people. Nowadays, they had to learn to live like—like show people!

With the sheet still over his face, Judge Larwell stirred in his bed. He became aware of the silence in the house and aware that it was being imposed for his sake. He had not got to bed till after 6 a.m. Suddenly he threw back the sheet, to see what time it was now. The window shades were drawn, and so he had to put on a light to see the face of the clock. Then, when he saw what time it was, it didn't seem to matter. He reflected only that he couldn't have imagined he would really sleep so soundly after last night. When he was leaving the hotel, someone asked if he were not going to get up to catch the morning television reports. They simply weren't able to believe that he would want to sleep through such a morning.

On the bedside table, he read the notes he had scribbled to himself as he was getting into bed. "Oh, Lord!" he exclaimed, reaching for the telephone. But the telephone was dead, of course, being off the hook downstairs. He jiggled the instrument several times. Then suddenly none of it seemed so all-fired urgent. Besides, Jake Ransom, the PR man, and Miss Ledbetter and Billy Henderson and his son-in-law Joseph would go on looking after things, as they had throughout the campaign. The great trick had been turned. They had won! Now he could hold the world at arm's length for a few hours—the very world he had been courting yesterday. Now he could relax for a while.

Yet suddenly it was the silence of the house itself that seemed real to him above anything else and that demanded his full attention. Somehow, he felt he couldn't bear it, could never bear silence of that sort again. Pulling on his robe, he went into the hall and listened for some sound of life. Hearing none, he moved on to the head of the stairs. Still only the silence, the unspeakable, intolerable silence of this private house. All at once he threw back his head and called at the top of his campaign-roughened but still powerful voice: "I—am—hun—gree!"

Mrs. Larwell appeared in the doorway from the living room and stood at the foot of the stairs. She was smiling up at him. It was a good sign if he was hungry. It meant he had not fixed his mind on her yet. The cook could give him his breakfast—or lunch—and she could finish paying last month's bills. "I'll tell Nola you're up," she called. "Would you like to have her bring you something on a tray?"

"I would not," he replied, clearing his throat. Then, striking a Napoleonic pose, slipping his hand inside his plaid robe and dropping his chin onto his bare chest, he intoned, "The governor does not choose to eat alone."

Mrs. Larwell laughed obligingly. She recognized his elated mood and knew, of course, that that was what she could have expected today. "All right," she said. "Is it breakfast or lunch you want?"

"Half and half," he announced solemnly from the head of the stairs, still holding the pose and fixing her with a simulated frown.

"Very well. I'll tell Nola. And while you get yourself dressed, I'll finish a little job I've begun in here."

Mrs. Larwell turned back to the living-room doorway. There were not many governors-elect, she reflected, who could and would sleep till two on this day. It was very healthy and youthful of him to be able to do so. She had known without asking, of course, what he would want to eat—tomato salad, a ham sandwich and scrambled eggs, with perhaps dry cereal for dessert—and she had known, as well, that he would not want to eat alone. Moreover, she knew that he would wish to get fully dressed before going downstairs. It was one of his old-fashioned, formal traits that he would never go down in his nightclothes. She was glad of that, too, because now it would allow her a few more minutes to work on her bills and perhaps even get started on a letter to one of her two old aunts. Her personal correspondence was, as a matter of fact, in worse need of attention than her bills.

But she was hardly through the doorway and in the living room before she heard him call again. He simply called her name: "Nell!" She heard him clearly, but at the far end of the long living room her little spinet desk beckoned to her. No, not the desk itself so much as the stack of bills with their address panes, and her own business envelopes in the half-open drawer, and the checkbooks spread out on the surface of the desk, and even the tiny roll of stamps and her own stick-on return addresses. They held out their arms to her, like so many little children.

But Mrs. Larwell knew where her first duty lay. She knew that some secretary could take care of her personal bills and even her personal correspondence in the future. The small satisfaction of writing those checks and scratching the bills off her list was not important. What difference did those bills make? She heard the voice at the top of the stairs asking, "Do you know where my new tattersall shirt is? I want to wear it with my blue suit." Yes, some secretary would have to take care of her personal bills in the future.

Presently she was walking quickly up the stairs. And she was wondering, Would it come now? Would he speak to her now of his appreciation for her joining in the campaign when she had hated it so? She stopped for a moment and then went to the kitchen to put the telephone on the hook and to tell Nola that Judge Larwell was ready to eat something now. Then she started upstairs again. And again the question filled her mind: Would it come now? How she longed to postpone the moment when he would try to speak to her of it! How she dreaded the moment! And yet she could not say why she did.

When she got upstairs, she found him rifling through the drawers of the big, old-fashioned chiffonier that had once belonged to her father. He was going through it like a burglar looking for money or jewels hidden among the clothes.

When she went into the room, he faced her momentarily in the wide mirror above the chiffonier and asked in a suspicious voice, "Where is it?"

"Where's what, dear?"

"The new tattersall shirt you bought me. I've decided that's what I ought to wear today—and with the blue suit."

"It's on the closet shelf, where I always put your new shirts."

He started toward the closet. He had already removed his robe and the top of his paisley pajamas. He now wore only the pants, which were tied with a drawstring around his narrow hips and over the sizable, low, and rather assertive belly he had developed in recent years. His narrow hips and long legs made him still look decidedly athletic, despite his belly, and in his present garb he looked like anything but his wife's idea of a governor of the state. Seeing him still in that wide mirror made it all too easy for her to remember how her father had appeared at such moments..

Her revered papa would have stood before her in a dark silk dressing gown, or if she had, as a little girl, burst into the room unexpectedly, she might have found him in his billowing white nightshirt, clipping his mustache before the mirror. *That* was how a governor should look in the privacy of his bedchamber. Yet here was this youngish-looking man, who, though already a grandfather, still played tennis and handball and sailed his own sloop on the reservoir lake. And whereas Papa had grown his mustache to make himself look old enough to be governor, *her* husband had often, during the campaign, gone about with his stomach sucked in, so that he would look even more boyish than he naturally did.

And in the chiffonier mirror, Mrs. Larwell saw herself, still a good-looking woman, who had kept her figure (because it was required of her) and whose pancake make-up and frosted hair deceived some people into thinking she was perhaps fifteen years younger than she was and certainly fifteen years younger than she sometimes felt. They were a handsome-looking pair, no doubt about it, and that was what politics *demanded* of you nowadays. It was a far cry from the way it once was, and a far cry from the way she had imagined it would be if ever her husband should occupy the gubernatorial chair.

She followed him to the closet, where he had pulled the new shirt from the shelf and was removing the pins. She took out his navy-blue pinstripe suit and began flicking off particles of lint. This was the sort of thing she liked doing for him. No matter how many servants she might have, she liked looking after his everyday needs, and as long as he was practicing law and later when he was on the bench, she had liked listening to his accounts of his courtroom battles and of the judgments he had to make—liked it especially when he said or implied that she was not really supposed to follow or understand all he told her.

Now she handed him the blue suit and took from him the shirt and the four round-head pins he had already pulled out of it. She placed the pins, points first, between her lips and proceeded to extricate the other pins from the folds of the shirt. Then, with all the pins between her lips and after removing the tissue paper and cardboard liner from the collar, she gave the shirt a good shaking, as if to shake out all its stiff newness. She eyed it critically and mumbled through the pins: "Mibb-ee I sh'ld give thizz crisses a few strocks wi' th' i'on."

Her husband understood her perfectly. Talking with pins in her mouth was something she had always seemed to relish. He glanced over his shoulder at the shirt she was holding up and shrugged. "I wouldn't bother," he said. He had laid his suit on the big double bed and was once again looking over the memoranda he had written himself last night, at the bedside table. "The phone is off the hook downstairs," he commented, in a relatively unconcerned tone.

"No," she corrected him. "I put it back on just before I came up."

"Ah," he said, with somewhat more interest, and he reached for the receiver. But then he shrugged again and didn't take it up.

She methodically and with evident satisfaction—even pleasure—unbuttoned the shirt buttons for him, even those at the cuffs. She was placing the shirt beside the suit on the bed when suddenly she changed her mind. "No," she mumbled, still through the pins. "I b'lev I'll j'st touch it up." She took the shirt and turned to go across the hallway to the little sewing room, where her ironing board was kept set up. There was an ironing board in the basement laundry and another in the kitchen, but she was a woman who would always have to have an ironing board of her very own and have to have it handy. She left him still standing at the bedside table, pulling a white undervest over his head.

The iron had to be plugged in and warmed up before she could begin pressing the creases out of the new shirt. Draping the shirt over the back of a straight oak chair, she moved toward the sewing machine. Her sewing machine was even more important to her than her iron and was always kept open, with only a little square of India print thrown over it as protection against dust. She moved toward the sewing machine now with the intention of sticking the pins, which she still carried between her lips, into the big strawberry pincushion there.

Instead, however, her attention was caught by several skirts and dresses of her own that were lying on the cutting table nearby. They had been lying there for many weeks, and her purpose had been to shorten the hems. One of her daughters had said to her once, "If you became Queen of England, you would still take up your own hems." And the other daughter had added, "Yes, and wash out your own bathtub." On that occasion, as on others, she had quoted her own mother to them: "There are some things that a lady will always do for herself."

She noticed that on the tweed and flannel skirts she had already marked with chalk where the new hem was to be folded. Inadvertently, almost, she took up the brown tweed skirt and, using the pins she held in her mouth, began pinning the new hem in place. Just as she had taken the last pin from her mouth, she heard a familiar creaking sound and realized that the iron was ready for use. She hesitated a moment, holding the warm woolen material between her thumb and forefinger, enjoying the sensation, relishing the feel of its texture on her fingertips. Then she stuck the last pin firmly into the skirt and moved directly to the more urgent business of ironing her husband's new shirt.

She finished with the iron after only two or three minutes. But when she had removed the electric plug and hung the shirt on a hanger, her attention was caught once again by the skirts to be hemmed. Returning to the cutting table, she could not resist taking up a paper of pins and continuing to pin the hem of the brown tweed.

When she had it in place all around, she held the skirt to her waist and observed it in the long mirror on the closet door. It was shorter than the skirt of the dress she wore, but it was the fashionable length this year. She had been conscious all through the campaign that her skirts were a little longer than was fashionable; but since she was on the platform so much, she thought it more becoming to a woman of her age to wear them somewhat longer than fashion prescribed. But now that the campaign was over, of course, she would feel free to conform to feminine fashion once more.

Putting aside the tweed skirt, she took up a gray flannel skirt, and hardly knowing what her fingers were doing, she began pinning the hem in place. Her fingers functioned rapidly and with great precision in such work, and she had got nearly halfway around the hem when suddenly the door from the hall was pushed open and Judge Larwell strode into the room. He had on his blue trousers, was wearing his shoes; he had even shaved.

"Ah," he said, seeing his shirt on the coat hanger beside the ironing board.

She raised her eyes, though continuing to push the pins into the soft flannel, and she said, "I'm sorry. Were you waiting for it? I got involved in this. Does it look all right, the shirt?"

"It looks great, but you shouldn't have bothered." As he was getting into the shirt and moving back toward the door to the hall, he asked casually, "What are you doing there?"

"Oh, I'm just pinning up these hems. I'm going to whip them in today. This has all been lying here for weeks." She glanced up to see him standing in the doorway with his eyes fixed on her.

Suddenly lowering his eyes, instead of letting them meet hers, he began slowly buttoning his shirt. Even before he spoke, she perceived that he was irritated. "Couldn't you get someone else to do that?" he asked.

"Silly, I like doing it. Taking up a few skirts is nothing."

"It's time-consuming, though—that sort of little job is. One has to learn to delegate such work," he said.

Then he was gone from the doorway. And it was as though he had given her an explicit order to put down her sewing and follow him. Also, it was somehow as though she were working in an office somewhere, as though she had been widowed and had had to go to work in a man's world and would have to try to forget that she had brought up two children and try to forget—that is, try not to "dwell upon" the fact—that she had known those many happy years of keeping house and entertaining for and being cherished by an affectionate husband.

As she left the sewing room, she gave one glance backward. The room seemed unreal to her quick glance, like a room she was remembering fondly if somewhat indistinctly from a long-ago childhood. She felt a lump in her throat. And then she laughed at herself. Why, what were a few skirts to her?

When she went back into the bedroom, he accused her frankly of trying to avoid him this morning.

"This afternoon, you mean," she said, laughing at him. And she went over and kissed him, saying, "How silly can a governor-elect be?"

He returned her kiss and smiled at shamefaced smile.

But as they went down the stairs, arm in arm, she wondered if she hadn't, after all, been avoiding him. Because now she was consciously dreading it again, the moment when he would thank her for her part in the campaign. When would it come? Or perhaps he was going to spare her. Oh, what *did* she mean by such silly nonsense? she asked herself. Yet the possibility that he was not going into the matter lifted her spirits almost magically.

She began to chatter about the three newspaper photographers who had been perched all morning, like three big birds, on the fenders of cars across the street, and about how everyone knew the judge had vowed, win or lose, to sleep all day on the day after the election, and about how faithfully Joseph, their son-in-law, had been guarding the front door, greeting people who came but turning them away. Now, she said, they must make Joseph come in and have brunch with them.

In the breakfast room, she found that Nola had places set for three. Somehow overlooking this obvious fact, she called through the kitchen doorway for Nola to set additional places for herself and Joseph.

"Yes'm, I already have," replied Nola cheerfully.

"Oh, yes, I see you have." And Mrs. Larwell detected in her own voice an absurd, resentful note. She ought to have been glad, she told herself, that the cook could guess she and Joseph would wish to have a bite while the judge ate. But she was so keenly, so painfully aware of being out of touch with the operation of her own kitchen and household that she had a *silly, silly* sense of being superseded. Nola had even sent Horace, the yardman and chauffeur, who had been guarding the back door, around to the front porch to invite Joseph to come in.

And presently Joseph appeared, his face flushed from being out in the autumn weather all morning and his manner all smiles and congratulations.

"List, oh, list!" began Joseph, sitting down at the breakfast table. "Really, you would hardly believe how many important folks have tried to force their way past me this morning. Ah, I could tell thee a tale!"

Joseph was considered quite literary and had even helped the judge with the wording in a good many of his speeches, though Mrs. Larwell was not always sure that his additions and corrections were beneficial. Sometimes in the middle of a speech, she had recognized Joseph's words on the judge's lips, and somehow from that point on, the speech would not ring true to her.

Her own father had never allowed anyone to tamper with his speeches, and to him the very idea of hiring a ghost writer—an idea the judge had recently been entertaining—would have been abhorrent.

Still, Joseph was a loyal admirer of the judge's, and that had to be appreciated. The other son-in-law, out in California, was an engineer and was openly scornful of politics and politicians. But Joseph had been at the judge's side throughout the campaign, had been there, in fact, at times when his mother-in-law had thought he ought to be at home with his pregnant wife. During these same months, the daughter in California had also been pregnant, and the engineer had given this as their excuse for not coming home for the election. Well, at any rate, Joseph had not slept at all last night and had been on the front porch this morning, protecting the judge's well-earned right to rest.

"You just couldn't believe," Joseph said now, "how little consideration some of these fellows show for a man who has fought the hard campaign you have, or how little respect, in fact, they have for the office of governor of this state. I really don't believe I could have kept them out if those two troopers hadn't been there with me. One newspaperman pretended he had a note to you from Senator Brice, and when I asked to see the note, he just laughed in my face and walked away—wadding up the paper and stuffing it in his pocket."

The judge laughed pleasurably at Joseph's reporting of this last little incident. "Well, I'm afraid that's how it's going to be from here out," he declared. "The campaign was nothing to how it will be now. I'll be needing you all the way, Joseph. I don't know what your title will be, but I'll be needing you to keep such fellows off my back."

"Oh!" exclaimed Mrs. Larwell, interrupting suddenly. "I should think your secretaries and the state troopers together could do that, without taking up your own son-in-law's time."

There was an asperity in her words that she had not intended should be there and that seemed to draw her husband's attention entirely away from Joseph. She saw him drop his eyes from Joseph to the plate that Nola had just set before him and then lift them to her own face. It was a trick of his she had often observed in the past. She had observed that, in any conversation, he seldom moved directly from one important subject to another. That is, there was always an effort to prevent your detecting the mental associations he made or the logic of his transitions. She had always acknowledged to him that he was too subtle and too deep for her; but there *were* moments when she had consciously to conceal from him her knowledge of his depths and subtleties.

"Nola!" she called over her shoulder, turning her face away from him and toward the kitchen. "Give us luncheon forks, please, and not these big dinner forks. Nola!" But there was no answer from the kitchen.

"Nell, darling, I don't—" began the judge.

But she pretended not to hear him. Although she and Joseph, as well as the judge, had already been served, she snatched the forks from beside their plates. And rising from her chair, she set out for the kitchen. Nola was nowhere to be seen. After serving them, she had no doubt stepped to her room for a moment. Or she might, so far as her mistress knew, have put on her hat and coat and left the house forever! *That* was how little Mrs. Larwell felt she knew of what her own cook might do nowadays.

"Nola!" she called again. And the silence she got for answer somehow made her think of the names of other cooks she had had over the years. She was tempted, almost, to stand there calling their names: "Minerva! Gertrude! Maybelle! Clara!" Nola seemed no less someone out of the past than they.

But realizing that her husband and her son-in-law were waiting for their forks, Mrs. Larwell scurried back through the breakfast room and into the dining room. She went there to fetch the luncheon forks. But where were they? She had pulled open the top, shallow drawer of the buffet and found that they were not in their accustomed place. *Where* could Nola have put them? It seemed incredible that she no longer knew where her own flat silver was kept.

She was tempted, almost, to return to the breakfast room and announce that Nola and the flat silver were missing. Instead, when she opened the swinging door and saw her son-in-law and her husband waiting there without forks, she quickly crossed over and put one of the dinner forks in Judge Larwell's hand.

He accepted it but simultaneously seized her free hand in his own. "Thank you," he said gently. "Thank you for the fork, my darling, and thank you for everything else." She saw him glance across the table at Joseph and heard him say, "She's been a wonderful campaigner, hasn't she, Joe?"

She knew his glance at Joseph meant nothing, and yet she had a sense of discovering a conspiracy between them. Only, of course, it wasn't merely between them. The whole world, somehow, was conspiring against her. She could feel the blood draining from her cheeks. It seemed she might actually faint.

"I never saw anything like it," Joseph was saying as he wrested his fork from her. "Boy, what a campaigner she turned out to be! The timid, reserved little Mrs. Larwell! I'll never forget that night at Lawrenceburg when the rest of us sat there tongue-tied, how she stepped up to the lectern and began: 'I plead guilty to the soft impeachment!' Until that night, I hadn't known my pretty little mother-in-law had such powers of rhetoric."

"It was a quotation I used," Mrs. Larwell said in a whisper, her voice trembling. She was remembering that wretched moment at Lawrenceburg, when it had seemed anything would be better than the silence. Someone in the crowd had called out a phrase used in one of the opposition papers that morning: "The genteel judge." She had felt he was being attacked for the decent good manners she had always encouraged in him. And this had happened on the very first night he had been able to persuade her to sit on the platform.

"What I won't soon forget," the judge was saying, "is the sight of her shaking hands with that line of mill workers at Cedar Point. When those old codgers and those young roughnecks, who had been heckling me only fifteen minutes before, saw who they were going to shake hands with, they came flocking from all over the plant." The judge held on to her hand now and gave it a series of squeezes as he spoke.

And it really was as if she were out there in the rain at Cedar Point again, wearing her rain hat and raincoat and shaking hands with all those young boys and old men. While she had stood there in the rain, it had come over her that there were no middle-aged men among the mill hands. There were only smooth-faced young boys, mixed with young boys who had at some point turned into rough-faced old men. Her heart had gone out unreservedly to those young boys and those old boys.

And afterward, at home that night, the memory that there had been no middle-aged men among them had touched her. But what had troubled her most, when she was alone that night, was the realization that she had shaken their hands with a genuine cordiality and she was not capable of a professional cordiality. She had acted on her real feelings, and the result was that the persons she had deceived that day were not the mill hands but her husband and her son-in-law and Miss Ledbetter and Jake Ransom and Billy Henderson.

"My darling Nell," the judge was saying now, still holding her hand and, though Joseph was present, addressing her in a language and tone that he had always heretofore reserved for their private exchanges, "my darling, you do have powers I never suspected you possessed. I owe you a debt that I can never repay, and the bad part is that I have no doubt that you will go on increasing that debt of mine so long as we live."

Mrs. Larwell burst into tears. With her own dinner fork clutched in one hand and with the judge holding on to her other hand, she began heaving and sobbing, the contorted features of her face completely exposed.

Now the moment had come. She had known how it would be without knowing she knew. What she had dreaded, what she had known to expect (without knowing she knew), was that his expression of gratitude would be but an expression of his desire, his will, that she not now discontinue her public role. Tears quite literally flooded her eyes and flowed down her cheeks. It was as though, quite literally, some dam within her had burst. She knew that there was no turning back and no answering him.

As he came to his feet and looked directly into her eyes, she felt a flash of hatred for him. She remembered his saying to Joseph at some point in the campaign, "Do only small favors for others on the ticket, and ask only large ones." She hated him—but only for the one moment. She loved him; he was her life. But her life would be changed now. The world was changed now, however, and it was only that she must change with it. *Everybody* had to change with the times. And it was her duty to him to change. *Politicians no longer had to learn to live like rich people; they had to learn to live like show people.* Somehow, she would learn.

The judge had his arms about her, and Joseph had come around to her, too. They were calling her a perfect darling. They were touched that she should shed tears over his expression of gratitude.

Beyond Joseph's tear-blurred silhouette, she had an even more blurred glimpse of the kitchen and saw that Nola had returned and was in command there. Drying her eyes and cheeks on a napkin the judge had handed her, Mrs. Larwell said, "I'm being *so* silly. How silly *can* a woman be? The wife of the governor-elect! This should be the happiest day of our life, and I shouldn't spoil it with tears." Looking at her son-in-law, she said, with a baffled smile, "Many are called but few are chosen."

"Wonderful!" replied her literary son-in-law.

Then, to her husband, she said, "I'm through with crying now." And she went up on her toes and kissed him on his clean-shaven cheek.

Then the three of them sat down to their brunch, busying themselves with their large dinner forks. And it seemed to the wife of the governor-elect that she was quite literally through with crying, that she might never shed another tear as long as she lived.

Voiceplace

George Ella Lyon

EARLY in "Song of Myself," Walt Whitman declares that he is "one of the Nation of many nations, the smallest the same and the largest the same" and then gives us fourteen long lines of places and ways of life, from the "Kentuckian walking the vale of the Elkhorn" to the fishermen "off Newfoundland, / at home in the fleet of iceboats." He concludes the catalogue by saying: "I resist any thing better than my own diversity, / Breathe the air but leave plenty after me, / And am not stuck up, and am in my place."

Whitman knew that democracy did not require and should not produce sameness—even within the individual ("Do I contradict myself?" he asks. "Very well then I contradict myself"), that in fact our strength and vitality spring from our variety. No melting pot for Whitman, no stew even, but many pots aromatically bubbling with everything from grits to borscht to fricasseed buffalo. What has happened to our taste for differences?

"I hungered for the burr of Appalachian r's," writes West Virginia poet Mary Joan Coleman in "D.C. Working Girl Lonesome." Living in the city, she longed not only for the place but for the *voice* of home. She grew up where the ruggedness of landscape and life shaped the language, where metaphors outnumbered even kinfolks. Having moved to a place where her accent was ridiculed, she realized her loss. For the history and spirit of a place are in its voices; to accept the denigration of the speech you were born into is to sever one of the threads of ongoing life.

It is also to foster the false impression that culture happens somewhere else, New York or Los Angeles, Chicago or Boston, and has to trickle down to the rest of us, that culture is a commodity that we buy or travel far to see rather than something that comes *from* us and speaks *to* us. It implies that stories—and therefore the people who tell and hear them—are more important in the metropolis than in the mountains or the Midwest.

It took me a long time to recognize the vital connection between voice and place in my own life and work. I grew up in Harlan County, Kentucky, in the coalfields, and was in high school during the War on Poverty. I remember the TV stereotypes—not just on *The Beverly Hillbillies* but on the news—of mountain people both materially and culturally deprived. So I thought, if I am going to write, the first thing I have to do is go somewhere and acquire a culture. During that process I would learn to sound like I was from somewhere else. I didn't know that was like cutting your throat to remedy hunger.

In college I wrote poetry primarily, and my subjects were medieval music, Dutch painters, and love. The language was that of a person born in a book and majoring in men's studies. We called it English. But I kept a journal, too, where I set down things that interested me. One was a sentence I'd seen printed in crayon on a young child's paper at Pine Mountain Settlement School: "I hope how soon Spring comes." I loved the way the rising sap of spring, hope itself, lifted the words into a new order. Not standard but rare, expressive. "How I hope Spring comes soon" is tired by comparison.

Another thing I took notes on was how my grandmother talked. "I feel like a stewed witch," she'd say. Or "I ain't seed you in a month of Sundays." I wrote down names of relatives she remembered: Honey-eating Richard, Pie-belly Miracle. I wrote down a story she told me of Old Aunt Martha Money who could cure the summer complaint. I didn't put this into poems. I just collected it. Poems, as far as I knew, didn't have stuff like that in them. But I valued the live language and elemental nature of her stories. Let not thy left brain know what thy right brain is doing.

After graduating from Centre College and the University of Arkansas, I studied with Samuel Yellen and Ruth Stone at Indiana University. It was exactly what I needed. Not just the workshop, but the community of writers that it fostered. Among those friends the most immediately important to me was Michael Allen, an Ohio poet who wrote about Sunday dinner at his grandmother's, about growing corn, about everyday things that he knew as well as his face. I was astonished. Could I do that? Why not? Ruth's class added to this realization the fact that it was not only possible but crucial to write out of my experience as a woman. Suddenly I had a wealth of material. In the twenty years since then, I've been trying to figure out how to be true to it.

Where you're from is not who you are, but it's an important ingredient. I believe you must trust your first voice—the one tuned by the people and place that made you—before you can speak your deepest truths. Irish poet Seamus Heaney, recent winner of the Nobel Prize, confirms this, saying in a radio interview, "I think for words to have any kind of independent energy, in some way they have to be animated by the first place in ourselves. Until that happens, words don't have that freedom and conviction that you need to write poems." We see, then, that if a person's experience of the written voice confirms her "first voice"—both in what she reads and in how she is taught to write—then her growing literacy will be fed by strong cultural roots.

As an Appalachian, my education to this possibility was continued by discovering Jeff Daniel Marion's literary magazine *The Small Farm* in 1975 and *Appalachian Journal* the year after. Danny and I began corresponding, and I found out there was a whole passel of people out there writing down how their grandmother talked and why she talked like that and why her farm was taken away from her. I found out there was an entire tradition of Appalachian writing; furthermore, some of the songs my daddy had sung to me were Child ballads. In short (though it wasn't short—it took years) I found out I had a culture. I'd been to college and graduate school, London and Paris, the Smithsonian and the New York Public Library, and now I needed to go home. For while I found all sorts of necessary and wonderful things in those places, I couldn't find my voice.

I don't mean I went home literally—I'd been going back for holidays and summer visits all along—I mean I went home inside; I began to pay attention to all those voices, to the language and people I grew up with. In doing so, I abandoned the larger culture's belief that such voices had no place in art, had, in fact, nothing to say.

Kurt Vonnegut says that he finally realized he had to sound like a person from Indianapolis because that's what he was. No construct, no posture could give him as convincing a voice. This doesn't mean, of course, that he had to write about Indianapolis; it doesn't even mean that someone picking up *Slaughterhouse Five* would know he's from Indianapolis. It means Vonnegut did a countercultural thing: he took that voice seriously enough to believe it could speak to us all. Never mind that it's not from a designated cultural area. It's an ordinary voice. An ordinary voice given to visions. . . .

Each place exists in context and in contrast with others and I grew up not only in Harlan, but in not-Lexington, not-Dayton, not-Orlando. I grew up where the Greyhound bus did not go through but turned around and went back. It was not because, as jokes would have it, we were so bad that nobody wanted to go farther; it was because the road through to Virginia was a cross between a washboard and a roller coaster.

I didn't grow up *in* Harlan either, but four miles south, in a neighborhood bounded on two sides by the Cumberland River, one side by the railroad, all sides by mountains, and called Rio Vista. I'd like to know how that sudden Spanish got there.

I think being rooted nourishes a person. It limits you, too, the way all actuality limits possibility. But it gives you a context, a tapestry of conditions and stories into which your story will be woven and from which you can follow the thread of others. My metaphor for writing is listening—perhaps in part because I had visual problems as a child—but I couldn't do it if I didn't have a choir, a cacophony, a family reunion of voices in my head. Totally fictional voices speak out, too. Part of my work is extending the invitation.

Just as I know we are all mortal, all bound to drop out of that reunion one by one, I also know that the spirit survives. This is my experience. It came to me naturally in childhood, before I could read or write, but it's taken me many years as a writer, as an adult, to find my way back to it. I cannot give you any doctrine, only testimony. Places have spirits; they haunt us as they are haunted by the lives that have been lived in their shelter, on their ground.

from

Parable of the Talents

Henry Louis Gates, Jr.

TWENTY-FIVE years ago, I left West Virginia for Yale University, to join the blackest class in the history of that ivy-draped institution. I drove up on my own, without my parents. They were never comfortable in that island of leaded glass and Gothic spires, although you might say they spent much of their lives making sure I arrived there. My father worked two jobs—loading trucks at a paper mill, plus a night shift as a janitor for the phone company—to keep us well fed and well clothed, and to pay the premiums on "college insurance policies," a thousand dollars when we reached eighteen. It never occurred to me that we might be poor until much later a sociologist told me so, pinpointing "the Gateses" in a mass of metallic-tasting demographics that left me numb with the neatness of it all.

I suppose that Yale represented both a betrayal and a fulfillment of their dreams. Blacks are wedded to narratives of ascent, to borrow a phrase from literary critic Robert Stepto, and we have made the compounded preposition "up from" our own: up from slavery, up from Piedmont, up from the Bronx, always up. But narratives of ascent, whether or not we like to admit it, are also narratives of alienation, of loss. Usually the ascent is experienced not as a gradual progression but as a leap, and for so many of my generation that leap was the one that took us from our black homes and neighborhoods into the white universities that had adopted newly vigorous programs of minority recruitment. It should be said that the adjustment was a two-way street: we were as strange to the institutions in which we found ourselves as those institutions were to us. In short, we were part of a grand social experiment—a blind date, of sorts. We weren't a tenth, of course; and whatever talent we had wasn't necessarily greater than our compeers who were passed over, or who opted out; but we were here. You might call us the cross-over generation.

To speak in strictly chronological terms, we are among the late-boomers who now occupy the White House and the Congress—an age grade that includes Bill Clinton and Robert Reich and William Kristol. But the sense of generational affinity is intensified within the race: ours was the first generation to attend integrated schools in the wake of *Brown v. Board;*[1] to have watched, as children, the dismantling of Jim Crow and to wonder where the process might end; to be given the chance, through affirmative action, to compete against white boys and girls; to enter and integrate the elite institutions just as the most expansive notions of radical democracy made an entrance.

I picked Yale almost out of a hat. After a year at a junior college near my home, a place where "nigger" was hung on me so many times that I thought it was my name, I decided to head north, armed with a scholarship and a first edition of Strunk and White's *The Elements of Style.*

By day—and it was still light when I first arrived in New Haven—the university is a tangible, mortar-and-stone manifestation of an Oxonian ideal of Gothic perfection. By night, the sense of enchantment increased: the mammoth structures, strangely out of keeping with the surrounding town, guarded their streets with bearded shadows made by the half-light of the lamp-posts. At Yale, battle hymns were Congregational, with delicate changes of key. The building that just *had* to be the college cathedral turned out to be Sterling Library. Every feature of the place was alarming and exhilarating. Welcome to Never-Never Land, I told myself. This is your world, the world you've longed for and dreamed of. This was where the goods and entitlements of the American century were stored and distributed. It was the grown-up version of the world of Captain Midnight Decoders; the repository of all those box tops I used to ship off to Kellogg's in fair exchange for laser guns. If college was a warehouse for what we've modishly learned to call "cultural capital," the question wasn't how to get it but what to do with it. . . .

SO it was a period when the belief in progress seemed more than wishful thinking. Certainly my parents never allowed my brother or me to doubt that we could become whatever we chose. Nor did they let us doubt that the world would yield its secrets if only we turned our attention to it. They were not surprised by their children's attainments. I do not know if they loved America, but they shared the hopeful vision of America

1. **Brown *v.* Board:** Case in which, on May 17, 1959, the U.S. Supreme Court ruled unanimously that racial segregation in public schools was unconstitutional.

that the Princeton political scientist Jennifer Hochschild has analyzed in an invaluable 1995 study as the ideology of the "American dream." That is, they believed in the possibility of upward mobility, of racial betterment, of collective progress. They believed that America was in part malign, but that it was not entirely malign. They believed that the agency of black folk was circumscribed by circumstance, but that black folk had agency all the same. They knew that white folk had the power; but they believed that power was a shifting, fluid thing, like mercury, and that some of it was always seeping away, puddling up before somebody else. They knew that black folk had gone through bad times, but they also let themselves believe, or at least half-believe, that times they were a-changin'.

The vision of the world they shared was one in which both our purpose and our enemies were clear. We were to get just as much education as we possibly could, to stay the enemies of racism, segregation, and discrimination. (If we heard it once, we heard it a thousand times: education is the one thing nobody can take away from you.) By my first year of school, at the Davis Free School in Piedmont, West Virginia—which had integrated just one year before I entered—I understood in some deep part of me that all that was being asked of me was to pay attention. We never once were allowed to doubt that we were special. And only sometimes did we allow ourselves to wonder why.

It was a world in which comporting ourselves with dignity and grace, striving to "know and test the cabalistic letters" (as Du Bois[2] put it) of the white elite—but also acknowledging and honoring those of us who had achieved—was central to being a colored person in America: so we were given to understand. And indeed, back when Du Bois was the editor of *The Crisis* magazine, he published the portraits of black college graduates, lawyers and doctors, on its cover and in its pages. Law and medicine, education and scholarship—these were the pinnacles of achievement, these the province of the Talented Tenth. I don't claim that we ever lived up to this idealized image. But at least these were the images, the ideals, that were presented to us. Once upon a time, our communal values and aspirations were intact. Only racism and segregation stood between our people and the fullness of American citizenship. If only we could secure our legal rights, the argument went, if only we could use the courts to strike down segregation; if only *de jure* segregation

2. Du Bois: W. E. B. Du Bois (1868–1963), U. S. historian, educator, and civil rights leader.

could be banished from the land once and for all—then all else would follow, as day upon night. The world was simple then; our enemy an easy target.

And then the obvious obstacles tumbled and fell. *De jure* segregation was killed off in the American judicial system. *Brown v. Board* was a triumph of decades of legal scholarship, under the leadership of such accomplished jurists as Charles Hamilton Houston, Thurgood Marshall, Constance Baker Motley—the list is long and noble. (How much went into the preparation of that brief before the Court—a rare collaboration between our legal practitioners and our scholars, between politicians and political activists, between whites and blacks, Jews and Gentiles, working together in an interracial compact that few of us can even remember, let alone imagine happening again.) Certainly the decade between *Brown* and the passage of the Voting Rights Act in 1965 was a time when the Negro felt more optimism than would have been justified in any other single decade in our century.

To be sure, the three years that followed were bloody and turbulent ones (you could think of these years as framed by the assassinations of Malcolm X and Martin Luther King, or by the riots in Watts in 1965 and the riots just about everywhere else in 1968, especially those surrounding the Democratic Convention in Chicago)[3] And yet despite all this, the grandchildren of the Talented Tenth—those who had been trained to succeed, geared to prosper, prepared by family and teachers to "cross over" into the white world once the walls of segregation came tumbling down—plunged headlong into the abyss of integration. . . .

The sort of institutions through which elites sustain themselves always seemed to inhabit an arcadia of their own, and yet somehow, in my mind, they always loomed like the clanking, infernal machinery of Fritz Lang's *Metropolis*. I should say that Yale wasn't my first encounter with one. I was in tenth grade when Exeter came about; a friend at a church summer camp told me about the place. Going to Exeter, you understand, was not something people in Piedmont knew about, not the way people at Yale "know" about Exeter. What *I* knew was that it was a place with a big library which offered a lot of courses. And in the main, that's what it was for me. An interview with the young Jay Rockefeller,

3. Assassinations of Malcolm X . . . Democratic Convention in Chicago: Malcolm X (1925–1965), U. S. political activist and leader in an Islamic movement. Dr. Martin Luther King, Jr. (1929–1968), U. S. Clergyman and leader in the civil rights movement. Watts 1965, Southwestern district in Los Angeles, California which gained widespread attention as a scene of racial violence. Democratic Convention in Chicago of 1968, scene of violence in which antiwar activists protested the convention and Hubert Humphrey's support of the Vietnam War.

an easy entrance exam, and a full scholarship later, I said bye-bye to Piedmont and drove with my uncle to the New Hampshire woods. My parents said their good-byes in Piedmont, as if there were a boundary they preferred not to trespass.

As quickly as Exeter came into my life, however, Exeter left; or rather, I left Exeter. Sometime in my first semester, I "up and decided" that it was past time for me to go back home. Dean Kessler checked my records what seemed to be a hundred times—my test scores were perfect, I had straight A's. There was no reason, he said. "Who gave you authority to leave?" he wanted to know. That's what settled it for me. I thought the knock on the door was just my classmate Joel Motley, whose room was next to mine. It was the dean, red-faced, angry, and a bit disappointed. I think he thought if he yelled at me, somehow I would cower my way back to French I-A. I gave up Exeter at that moment, staring blankly into his crimson, pockmarked face. "Think of our people," Joel, the soul of black insouciance, said that night. "Think of yourself. Where is Piedmont, anyway?" "I'll be back," I told him, and somehow knew I would, though I didn't mean Exeter, exactly. That was the first airplane trip I ever took. I still don't know for sure why I felt I had to leave; I think that Piedmont was just too far to fall back into, so I decided not to have to fall at all. Homesick for Piedmont, I went back, and soon became homesick for Exeter.

But I stayed at Yale; and I graduated, as a number of my friends did not, and I did so not as a matter of course but as a matter of will. I still remember that crucial first month, with daily sessions in the Linnonia and Brothers reading room, working out inorganic chemistry problems by the light of the low-wattage table lamps. I had convinced myself that at Yale I would be average; a C+ was what I was aiming for. Learning to speak out in class, always my forte before, now came slowly and painfully. But it was History 3-I that made the difference, in Burrell Billingslea's discussion group. Never have I put so much work and expectation, fear and care, into the preparation of a five-page paper. Had the returned grade been a Pass, or just a High Pass, the tenor of my years at Yale would probably have been as gray as a New Haven winter. But there it was, in unforgettable bright red letters: "Honors. Nice Paper." Fifteen students—eight seniors, four juniors, and a handful of others—and one Honors.

from

In Country[1]

Bobbie Ann Mason

In Country *tells the story of a teenaged Kentucky girl who wants to learn more about her father, Dwayne, who died in the Vietnam War before she was born. Sam lives with her Uncle Emmett who, like his friend Tom, also served in Vietnam. Emmett and Tom both suffer mentally from the traumas of war, and refuse to talk about their experiences. However, when Sam reads her father's diary she begins to understand his war experience and the meaning of his death.*

SAM was driving her new car on the back roads toward her other grandparents' farm. They had invited her to spend the night, and she had told Emmett not to expect her back until the next day. Mamaw and Pap Hughes lived far out in the country and she had not seen them in almost two years. She felt uneasy, but she loved having a car. Tom had advised her to record the mileage and get gas every two hundred miles. He said he had worked with the gas gauge, but it was a subtle mechanism, harder to repair than something obvious, like a carburetor or a muffler.

All the men she knew fiddled with gadgets. They were always fixing something.

She passed the place her mother said looked like England. She was far out in the country, and soon she turned off on a smaller road. She passed old farms that looked unchanged since the time her father had lived out here. Irene had said Emmett was a country boy when he went to the war, but Dwayne was even more of a country boy. He rode a school bus to the county school fifteen miles from his house. He had met Irene at a basketball game. Irene and Emmett attended the city school, but they had to pay tuition because they lived outside the city limits. Now a consolidated county school was being built. Grandma Smith always said Irene had felt inferior in the city school because she was self-conscious about being from the country and

1. In Country: A term soldiers used to denote their tour of duty in the Vietnam War (1954–1975).

so she did rebellious things to get attention, like read the chapter with the boring list of begats as her Bible passage in homeroom. But Sam was proud that her mother had been so wild.

Sam had wanted to care about her father, but she didn't know enough about him. She wasn't even sure how her mother had felt about him, if she had really loved him. If Irene had begun to see the war was wrong, would she have started to blame him after he died? Sam didn't know. She didn't know how she felt about him either. She thought of Tom, and how she had wanted Dwayne to be like him. But Tom was old, and in his letters Dwayne was just a kid. Dwayne and Irene, a teenage romance. Sam had wanted to believe there was something magic between them that had created her and validated their love. But teenage romances weren't very significant, she realized now. Sam and Lonnie. Dawn and Ken. Sam had been told so often what a miracle it was that she came along to compensate for the loss of Dwayne. She knew she had been making too much out of the brief time her parents were married before he went overseas. During that month, she had originated. She didn't know why the moment of origin mattered. Scientists were trying to locate the moment of origin of the universe. They wanted to know exactly when it happened, and how, and whether it happened with a big bang or some other way. Maybe the universe originated quietly, without fireworks. Making a baby had nothing to do with love, or anything mystical, or what they said in church. . . .

The road meandered past an overgrown graveyard. Some new house trailers perched on blocks in bare fields. She passed through an abandoned settlement, with an old feed mill and a boarded-up store with a rusted Orange Crush sign. The Methodist church was whitewashed and had a newly graveled parking lot and a marquee on wheels that said KEEP THE CHRIST IN CHRISTMAS.

Mamaw and Pap lived up a narrow lane, which turned off a graveled road, with a new green sign, "Bob James Rd." She remembered that Bob James was one of the neighbors, a prosperous farmer with eleven children and several hundred acres. She wondered if having a road named after him meant he had died.

As Sam drove up, a speckled chicken skidded across the driveway in front of the car. She parked behind a green Cutlass. On the turnaround were a blue pickup, a battered black pickup, and a Pontiac. A brown hound in a pen roared.

They were expecting her, and Mamaw had dinner ready. Mamaw's daughter, Donna, was there with a baby in a blue romper suit. Somehow Sam never could think of Donna as her aunt. Mamaw's hair was pinned on top of her head, and she had on a dress with a design similar to the pattern of the chicken. She smelled like sweat and furniture polish.

"Are those chickens Barred Rocks?" Sam asked.

"No. They're Domineckers," said Mamaw, leading Sam through the back porch. The porch sagged, and it was cluttered with buckets and seeds and canning jars.

Pap lifted Sam up by her waist, the way he did when she was little. "I just wanted to see if I could still do it," he said, laughing. "My old bones is give out. I screek so."

"He's been down in his back," Mamaw said disapprovingly.

"But Sam's a beanpole," Donna said, regarding Sam with a curious air of disdain. "I could lift her with one finger."

They were filled with questions about Irene's new baby—her teeth, her hair, her weight—and they supplied comparisons to Donna's little boy. Donna wanted to know why Sam didn't go with her mother to Lexington.

"You mean you're still living with your crazy uncle?" she said.

"Leave the child alone," said Mamaw. "If she went up there, look how she might turn out. I think it's fine when children want to stay where they was brought up. Bill Holsum's boy over yonder has to pay three hundred dollars just to fly home every Christmas. It's a shame. Bill never gets to see his grandchildren."

"Fred Turner's boy's in the Air Force and he's stationed in Rome, Italy," said Pap. "Talk about a fur piece from home."

"I saw on *That's Incredible* this miracle in Italy?" said Donna. "This nun had saved a saint's blood? The saint had been beheaded. And in a ceremony every year the dried blood turns to liquid. The scientists have checked it out and there's no way dried blood can liquefy, so it's a miracle. The one year it wouldn't liquefy was the year of all those earthquakes—1980."

"Law, I'd hate to live over there—with all those miracles they have," said Mamaw.

"They're religious," said Donna.

Mamaw set a platter of fried rabbit on the table. "This is swamp rabbit," she said.

"I shot it down in Cole's Bottom," said Pap. "It was the biggest one I ever saw. I had to pack it a mile."

Sam loaded her plate with two legs, mashed potatoes, brown field peas, green jello salad, and slaw. Donna mashed up peas for her baby, who had a scrawny face and hair like duck down. . . .

They talked about blue mold on their tobacco crop. Her other grandparents had a nicer house, Sam thought. The Hughes house had old linoleum and no dishwasher.

Mamaw drank some iced tea and said, "I could kick somebody. Back in December we could have signed up for five dollars a bushel for wheat, but Joe here had to wait and see what it would bring at harvest. He thought it might go higher, but instead wheat was so good this year the price went down, and we got three dollars and ten cents a bushel. So we liked eighty cents making three thousand dollars on the wheat, when we could have made five thousand."

"She's went on and went on," complained Pap. "How was I to know? You got to take a risk sometime."

"He could have signed up for a guaranteed five dollars a bushel back in December," Mamaw said.

"But who would have thought wheat would be so good this year?" Donna said brightly. "I'd have done the same thing."

As they ate, Sam was aware of the studio portrait of her father that was standing on the old oak dish cabinet. She remembered always seeing the picture there. He had longer, darker hair than he had in the picture she had at home, and no Army hat. He had on a blue suit. His face was tinted pink, like something an undertaker would do to a dead body. His hair had a slight curl at the middle of his forehead. She squinted her eyes and tried to see him at the table with them. He would be a grown man, like Tom. He wouldn't be like Tom, though, living in a garage apartment. He'd be discussing blue mold and whether to take risks on wheat prices. Irene wouldn't have gone to Lexington. Sam would be jiggling a baby on her knee, like Donna.

Donna and Mamaw were talking about Donna's sister-in-law, who had just moved into a new brick house with her husband and two children. Donna was raving about the house and all its appliances. "And that baby has everything you can name. Jean didn't take any hand-me-downs. And they've got a videocassette recorder and a bedroom suite that cost a thousand dollars. She doesn't think a thing about eating out."

Sam felt sick. She ate two slices of cake. It was white, with boiled icing, like something from Irene's white dinner, years ago.

After they ate, Mamaw showed Sam the pictures she had come to see. There were only a few besides the school pictures. She studied the small portraits, with "Burns High School" and the year printed below each one. He changed from a skinny, freckled little boy into a lanky, earnest teen-ager. Nowadays the school pictures were in color, and the kids posed in casual settings, by a swimming pool or under a tree, but these old-fashioned pictures were dark, cold, staring portraits. He was smiling in only two of them.

"This one's my favorite," Mamaw said, pointing to a picture in which his cowlick showed. "He was about sixteen there. He was the best boy! That was the year he made me that end table in shop."

"That was the year I was born," Donna said. "I don't have the slightest memory of him, my own brother. Ain't that a shame?"

Sam helped with the dishes. Pap was taking a short nap before he went back to work fixing some fences, and Donna was in her room with the baby. Her husband worked at Union Carbide, and they lived with Mamaw and Pap.

Sam set warm, dry glasses in the dish cabinet. The furniture-polish smell was in the cabinet. On top, her father stared down at her. She had looked at his likeness so often lately he was beginning to seem real, someone who might have some strong opinions about her.

Mamaw's hands didn't stop working at the dishes in the soapy water as she answered Sam's questions about Dwayne. She said, "You take after Irene's side of the family, Sam. You've got Dwayne's eyes, but you've got Irene's ways. And her cheekbones. I used to get so tickled at her. She'd do anything. She come out here once with Dwayne before they married, and she had a kite with her, and if she didn't go out in the pasture in her high heels and fly that kite I'm not here!" Mamaw laughed and dripped soapsuds down her elbows. "Dwayne was so taken with her. He thought she hung the moon."

"What did she think of him?"

"She was good to him." Mamaw swabbed a greasy plate with the dishrag. "Well, of course, he was my boy, but he was the thoughtfulest son you could ever have. That's a mother's privilege to think that, Sam. And he would have made a good farmer. Irene wanted him to go to New Orleans and work on a ship. Irene always wanted something big, anything to be different. But he wouldn't have done that. He would have come right back here. He was like that. He could talk about what-all he was going to do, but when it come down to it he was a mama's boy. He looked out for his mama and daddy. He wouldn't have gone off like Bill Holsum's boy did."

"He was a good boy," said Pap, appearing in the kitchen. "He never took a drink, didn't smoke."

"Did you get your nap out?" Mamaw asked him. "You wasn't laying down long."

"Y'all was beating your gums, and I couldn't sleep."

"Joe, tell Sam about Dwayne. She's here wanting to know more about her daddy. There's not a day I don't think of something loving he did. Like that flower box he made for Irene that time."

"He sure did love Irene," said Pap. "And I really do believe she loved him. Oh, they was young, and when you're that young you don't really know what you feel, but I saw how she was after the news come. It broke her heart."

"Irene was living at home with her folks then, and you was on the way, Sam. She was as big as a barn."

"We didn't see a whole lot of her," Pap said. "But after the news came they brought her over here, and everybody just set around and waited."

"It was so hard without the body," said Mamaw. "When somebody dies, you're supposed to prepare the body and watch over it. It's something that brings you all together, but he wasn't here. It was three days before we got him, and while we were waiting everybody was so lost. We just run around like a chicken with its head cut off. And the neighbors brought food. Oh, they just kept a-bringing good things to eat. It went on so long the people that brought food had to go home and cook some more for us. Lutie Cunningham brought a ham and a gallon of potato salad and three pies. I never will forget that. In a way, it was a relief when we finally got him in the ground." She laughed, a sort of whimper.

"It was a closed casket," Pap said. "The Army told us not to look."

Maybe it wasn't really him, Sam thought. Maybe he was still missing in action.

"That killed me," Mamaw said. "But they wrote and told what a help he was to his country. I take comfort in that."

"What good did he do for the country?" Sam asked. "Everybody knows it was a stupid war, but fifty-eight thousand guys died. Emmett says they all died for nothing."

"Well, Emmett can talk. He didn't die," Mamaw said indignantly. "Dwayne was fighting for a cause, and back then people didn't go around protesting. He believed in his country, and he was ready to go over there and fight."

"If you could go back to that time, would you let him go or would you send him to Canada?" Sam asked.

"Oh, Sam," Mamaw said, staring down at the linoleum. "People don't have choices like that."

"Did any stuff come with the body?" Sam asked. "I mean like his personal stuff. His clothes and things."

Mamaw nodded. "There wasn't much. I gave away the clothes, and I made Irene take the flag, but she wouldn't take anything else. I didn't understand that."

"Mom said there might be a notebook."

"There was a little diary. It's around here somewhere."

"Do you care if I have it?"

"I can't imagine what you want with it. There's not much in it. He told a lot more in his letters. He wrote the lovingest letters. I wouldn't take anything for them. But I'll look for that notebook when I get done here."

Sam went with Pap out to the barn to look for wire.

"What's wrong with that cat's ears?" she asked, pointing to a sore-eyed cat with scabby ears.

"I trimmed 'em. He had ear canker. If you trim it off, it'll heal, so I clipped about a quarter inch off of each one."

"I never heard of that."

"You do the same thing to rabbits. Why, I've seen cats with their ears trimmed down to a nub." He laughed, a hoarse chuckle. "Sam, you don't know nothing!" He took his work gloves, a hammer, and some nails from a tool shed next to the barn.

"Our cat never had ear canker," said Sam. "He's got fleas, though. They're about to drive Emmett crazy."

"That hound's got mange. I've got to mix up some sulfur and saltpeter and burnt crankcase oil and paint him when I get a chance," Pap said.

"Won't that kill him?"

"I doubt it. Sam, can you reach me them wire pliers on that shelf behind that sack of fertilizer?"

Sam was exploring in an old stall where she remembered her grandfather once raising a calf. This would have been where her father had raised calves when he was a boy. There were no cows here now. She handed Pap the wire pliers.

"We got too much fertilizer this year," he said, shaking his head.

Sam walked down a dusty lane with her grandfather. She was seeing the place her dad knew. She was seeing where her mother lived once for a few weeks, where Sam started growing in her belly. Her roots were here, and she had been here often enough for the place to be familiar, but not enough to really know it. She felt she was seeing it for the first time.

"I remember when Dwayne first brought Irene out here," Pap said. "She was just a skinny little squirt like you. Nothing embarrassed her. She went around asking me the name of everything. She got a kick out of Emma's hen-and-chickens cactuses, said they was like pincushions. Imagine that. She picked the biggest bunch of flowers. She went back in the fields along the fence rows and picked daisies and Queen Anne's lace and black-eyed Susans and I don't know what-all. I never would have thought of picking weeds like that. She was raised on a farm, so I was surprised she'd thought of picking them."

"She always liked flowers," Sam said. They were talking about Irene as though she were the one who had died, and when they talked about Dwayne they weren't specific. You should always be specific, Sam thought.

"Country kids are just like the city kids now," Pap said. "They've got more. And they have cars, so they can go running around. Used to, Saturday was when you went to town, but now they take off and go any day of the week."

They talked about Sam's new car for a while, and then Pap said, "Everybody always thought it was something that Dwayne left us such a gift. When you were born, I remember how proud everybody was." He hammered a nail into a fence post. "Everybody expected a boy, of course, but we loved you just the same."

"Everybody wished I was a boy," Sam said, crushing a clover head in her hand. "Did you know my daddy picked the name?" she asked. "He thought it was in the Bible."

"No. I didn't know that. Why, you learn something new every day. Well, I'll say!" He stroked his chin thoughtfully.

While her grandfather worked on the fence, Sam walked down by the creek. She had remembered some wild goose-plum trees in the creek. She found them, but she didn't see any fruit. The trees had honeysuckle vines on them. On a vine she saw a large green stinkbug with an orange spot and a figure eight on its back. Water striders pranced on the shallow pools of clear water in the creek bed. She used to call them Jesus bugs because of the way they walked on water. She looked around the farm, trying to see it in a new way, trying to see what her father had known, the world he knew before he went to Vietnam. These were his memories, what he took with him over there. She thought she could comprehend it. Everything he knew was small and predictable: Jesus bugs, blue mold, hound dogs, fence posts. He didn't know about the new consolidated county high school, rock video, *M*A*S*H.* He didn't know her.

At the house, the dog, outside his pen now, bowed lazily, then lay down in a patch of dirt he had dug in the shade near the flowerbed. His back was covered with scabs. Sam recognized many of the flowers—tall blue stalks, pink droopy flowers, big round yellow faces—but she had no names for them. The rosebushes were insect-eaten. The lilies had dried up. The August sun was beating down. Sam recognized a plant with seed pods forming from some of the flowers. She remembered that when they turned brown those seed pods would explode, scattering their seeds. She remembered the plant's name—touch-me-not.

"I found that diary," Mamaw called to Sam from the porch. "You can have it, but I don't reckon it'll tell you anything. He just set down troop movements and weapons and things like that. It's not loving, like the letters he wrote back. Those was personal. Irene didn't even want this little book, but you can have it if you want it."

Sam reached for the brown spiral notebook. Mamaw was standing on the porch, and Sam was below her on the steps. Sam remembered reaching just this way at graduation when the principal handed her the rolled diploma. But inside the ribbon was a blank piece of paper. The real diplomas were mailed later, because they had come too late from the printer.

Mamaw said, "I remembered that I couldn't even read all of it because I couldn't figure out his handwriting, so I don't expect it'll tell you anything, but at least you'll have something of his." She shooed a cat out the door. "Do you want us to take you out to the graveyard later?" Mamaw said.

"No, not today," Sam said, her eyes on the cat. "I've got to go somewhere."

"Whereabouts?"

"Paducah. I've got to go to Paducah."

If Snakes Were Blue

Robert Penn Warren

If snakes were blue, it was the kind of day
That would uncoil in a luxurious ease
As each mica-bright scale exposed a flange of gold,
And slowly, slowly, the golden eyes blinked.

It was the kind of day that takes forever—
As though minutes, minutes, could never be counted—to
  slide
Among the clouds like pink lily-pads floating
In a crystal liquid pure enough to drink.

And there was no distinction now between
Light and shadow except the mystic and faint
Sense of adaptation of the iris,
As light diminished and the first star shone,

And the last veery,[1] hidden in a thicket of alder,
Thought it would break its heart perhaps—or yours.
Let it be yours, then. For such gentle breaking
In that ambiguous moment could not be

Less than a blessing, or the kind of promise
We give ourselves in childhood when first dawn
Makes curtains go gold, and all night's dreams flood back.
They had guaranteed our happiness forever.

And in a way such promises may come true
In spite of all our evil days and ways.
True, few fulfillments—but look! In the distance lift peaks
Of glittering white above the wrath-torn land.

1. veery: A small, brown and cream-colored thrush.

Biographical Notes

A. R. Ammons (1926) was born outside Whiteville, North Carolina, in 1926. He started writing poetry while he was serving in the U. S. Navy during World War II. After completing his service, he attended Wake Forest University and in 1964 began teaching at Cornell University. Ammons is the author of nearly thirty books of poetry, among them *Collected Poems 1951-1971* and *Garbage* (1993), which both won the National Book Award; *Sphere* (1974), which received the Bollingen Prize. He has received fellowships from the Guggenheim Foundation, the MacArthur Foundation, and the American Academy of Arts and Letters. Since 1971 he has been Goldwin Smith Professor of Poetry at Cornell University.

Wendell Berry (1934) was born in New Castle, Kentucky. He graduated from the University of Kentucky where he received a B.A. and an M.A. degree in English. He later went to the creative writing Center at Stanford and taught creative writing for a year. While at Stanford, he wrote his first novel, *Nathan Coulter.* Wendell Berry has published over twenty works ranging from poetry, novels and fiction to essays, and biography. Wendell Berry now teaches English at the University of Kentucky where he lives with his wife and children on the farm where his family has lived since the early 1800's.

Doris Betts is the author of *Souls Raised from the Dead; Heading West,* and four other works of fiction. She is the recipient of the Medal of Merit for the Short Story, awarded by the American Academy of Arts and Letters, and is Alumni Distinguished Professor of English at the University of North Carolina at Chapel Hill.

William Wells Brown (1814–1884) was born a slave in Lexington, Kentucky. After twenty years in slavery, Brown escaped to freedom in January 1834. He married and moved to Buffalo where he began his career as an abolitionist. Brown, in his anti-slavery appeals, advocated the power of moral persuasion and rejected violence. Over the years, owing to his dedicated service, and his sophistication as a speaker, Brown's reputation increased leading to numerous appointments with anti-slavery societies, and a lecture tour of Great Britain. Brown was the first African American to publish a novel, *Clotel.* He is regarded as one of the most prolific black literary figures of the mid-nineteenth century.

Joseph Seamon Cotter, Jr. (1895–1919) was born in Louisville, Kentucky. He was raised in a strong family tradition of poetry. His father, an educator, wrote poetry himself, and the family maintained a close friendship with the prominent poet Paul Laurence Dunbar. After completing high school, Cotter attended Fisk University for two years, until he contracted tuberculosis and was forced to return home. Between the time he left college and his early death at the age of twenty-three, Cotter wrote continuously. The end result was the *Band of Gideon*, Cotter's only published collection of verse.

Donald Davidson (1893–1968) was born in Campbellsville, Tennessee. He received his B.A. and M.A. degrees from Vanderbilt University. After serving in World War I as an officer, he became a member of the Department of English at Vanderbilt University. Davidson is known for his outstanding dedication to his region and was one of the founders and leaders of the Fugitive and Agrarian movements at Vanderbilt. With Allen Tate, John Crowe Ransom, Robert Penn Warren and other Southerners, he contributed to *I'll Take My Stand* (1930), a significant work dealing with the problems of the South.

Henry Louis Gates, Jr. (1950) was born and raised in Mineral County, West Virginia. He graduated Phi Betta Kappa and *summa cum laude* from Yale College with a degree in history and was a London correspondent for Time magazine before receiving his Ph.D. in English from Cambridge University. He writes frequently for such publications as *The New York Times Book Review, The New Yorker,* and *The New Republic.* His books include *Colored People* (which won several national awards); *Figures in Black; The Signifying Monkey* (for which he received an American Book Award), and *Loose Canons.* He is now W. E. B. Du Bois Professor of the Humanities and chair of the Department of Afro-American Studies at Harvard University.

Janice Holt Giles (1909–1979) was born in Altus Arkansas. She received her formal education from the University of Arkansas, and moved to Louisville, Kentucky, in 1941 to work at the Louisville Presbyterian Seminary, where she met her husband, Henry Giles. The rural atmosphere of their home served as the inspiration for many of Janice Holt Giles's famous works—from her trilogy, *The Enduring Hills* (1950), *Miss Willie* (1951), and *Tara's Healing* (1951), novels embracing a simple life lived in country surroundings, to her historically based novel, *The Kentuckians* (1953) and *Shady Grove* (1967), a study of Appalachia during the 1960's.

Ellen Glasgow (1874–1945) was born in Richmond, Virginia. She was privately educated to a large extent by the books she read in her father's library. Her literary achievement is comprised of twenty novels written over a period of approximately half a century. She was awarded the Pulitzer Prize in 1942 for her novel *In This Our Life.* "Jordan's End," is taken from *The Shadowy Third* (1925), a collection of short stories.

Gail Godwin (1937) is a native North Carolinian and was raised in Asheville. She received a B.A. in journalism from the University of North Carolina at Chapel Hill; she holds a doctorate in modern letters from the University of Iowa. She has taught at the Iowa Writers' Workshop as well as at Vassar, and Columbia University. She is the author of nine novels and two collections of short stories. *The Old Woman* (1974), *Violet Clay* (1976), and *A Mother and Two Daughters* (1982) were nominated for National Book Awards. She is a Guggenheim Fellow and has received an Award in Literature from the American Academy of Arts and Letters.

Paul Green (1894–1981) was born near Lillington, North Carolina. As a youth he worked in the fields on his father's farm, in close contact with the laborers—people whom he would later portray in his folk dramas. He graduated from the University of North Carolina at Chapel Hill, and added to this two years of graduate work in philosophy at Cornell University, where he published his first volume of one-act plays. In 1923 he returned to the University of North Carolina to begin his teaching career as Professor of Dramatic Arts. As a writer, he has experimented with the short story and the novel as well as the drama, but his reputation rests primarily upon his plays. His most esteemed play is *In Abraham's Bosom,* which won Green the Pulitzer Prize for Drama in 1927.

Mildred Haun (1891–1966) was born in Hamblen County, Tennessee, to a large family who were primarily farmers. In 1931 she entered Vanderbilt University where as an undergraduate she met and was encouraged to write fiction by John Crowe Ransom and later by Donald Davidson. She completed most of her fiction writing before she had reached the age of thirty. In 1937, she compiled the traditional ballads and songs of Cocke County, and in 1940 published *The Hawk's Done*

Gone, a family chronicle told from the point of view of a mountain midwife.

George Ella Lyon (1949) was born and raised in Harlan Kentucky. She was educated at Center College, the University of Arkansas, and Indiana University, where she studied poetry. Her first book, *Mountain*, was published in 1983. Since then Lyon has published a second collection of poetry, *Catalpa* (1993), thirteen picture books, three novels for young readers, an autobiography, and many others. She has collaborated with such authors as Jim Wayne Miller and Gurney Norman, and is presently the executive director of the Appalachian Poetry Project. Lyon lives in Lexington with her husband and her two sons, and makes her living teaching and writing.

Bobbie Ann Mason (1940) was born in Mayfield, Kentucky, where her father was a dairy farmer. She graduated from the University of Kentucky in 1962 and worked in publishing magazines in New York. She received her M.A. from SUNY-Binghamton in 1966, and a Ph.D. in English from the University of Connecticut in 1972. Her first book of fiction, *Shiloh and Other Stories*, was published in 1982, and was awarded the Ernest Hemingway Award. Other works by Bobbie Ann Mason include *Spence + Lila* (1988) and *In Country* (1985), from which the present selection is taken.

Jim Wayne Miller (1936–1996) was born and raised in rural western North Carolina. He graduated from Berea College and in 1965 received a Ph.D. in German Language and American Literature from Vanderbilt University. He has taught throughout his career at Western Kentucky University. Jim Wayne Miller is a highly acclaimed promoter of Appalachian Literature, admired both as a poet and writer of prose fiction. He has published over twenty books.

Bill Moyers (1934) was born in Oklahoma and was raised in Texas. He began his journalism career at age 16 as a cub reporter on the *Marshall News Messenger*. In 1961, Moyers entered the world of television programming, working for public broadcasting stations and as a news analyst for CBS. During his twenty-five years in the media, Bill Moyers has received numerous awards, including thirty Emmy Awards, and in 1991 was elected a Fellow of the American Academy of Arts and Sciences. Four of Bill Moyers' books, based on his television series have become best sellers, including *Listening to America* (1971).

Elizabeth Madox Roberts (1881–1941) was born in Perryville, Kentucky, but spent most of her life in Springfield, Kentucky, where for over ten years she worked as a school teacher. At the age of thirty-six, Roberts enrolled as a freshman at the University of Chicago where her writing abilities matured; she graduated with honors earning a B.A. in English. She returned to Kentucky to write, publishing over seven novels, including the highly acclaimed *The Time of Man* (1926).

James Still (1906) was born in Lafayette, Alabama. He graduated from Lincoln Memorial University in Tennessee, where he was a fellow student of Jesse Stuart, and through scholarships was able to attend graduate school at Vanderbilt University and also at the University of Illinois. He moved to Hindman, Kentucky in 1932 and lived in a 150-year-old-cabin in the woods, a perfect setting for many of his most acclaimed works. Still wrote *Hounds of the Mountains*, *River of Earth*, and *On Troublesome Creek* all shortly after moving into his secluded cabin. These successful works and many other writings won him several awards, including the O Henry Memorial Prize, the Southern Authors' Award, and the American Academy of Arts and Letters Award.

Jesse Stuart (1906–1984) was born in W-Hollow in Greenup County, the son of an illiterate tenant farmer. He graduated from Lincoln Memorial University in 1929 and attended graduate school at Vanderbilt University. In the early 1930's, Stuart returned home to teach and administer schools. His success as a writer allowed him to quit teaching and eventually purchase the land on which his father farmed. Jesse Stuart was enormously prolific, writing over sixty works including poetry, stories and novels, as well as biography and autobiography. *Man With a Bull-tongue Plow* (1934), a volume containing over 700 sonnets, is generally considered the work which launched his career as a writer.

Joe Survant (1942) was born in Owenboro. After graduating from the University of Kentucky and the University of Delaware, he went on to teach at Western Kentucky University. His poems have been published in a number of magazines and anthologies. His most recent work *Anne & Alpheus 1842-1882* published in 1996 is a collection of sixty-four dramatic monologues, and won the 1995 Arkansas Poetry Award.

Peter Taylor (1917–1994) was born in Trenton, Tennessee. He studied at Vanderbilt University for one year, but transferred to Kenyon College in order to study under John Crowe Ransom.

He graduated from Kenyon College with a B.A. in 1940. He is the author of eight collections of short stories, several plays, and three novels—*A Woman of Means, A Summons to Memphis,* for which he won a Pulitzer Prize in 1986, and *In the Tennessee Country.* He was a member of the National Academy of Arts and Letters, and in 1984 he received a Senior Fellowship from the National Endowment for the Arts.

Robert Penn Warren (1905–1989) was born in Guthrie, Todd County, Kentucky, in 1905. He entered Vanderbilt University in 1921, where he became the youngest member of the group of Southern poets called the Fugitives, which included John Crowe Ransom, Allen Tate, Donald Davidson, and Merrill Moore, and which advocated the rural Southern agrarian tradition. From 1925 to 1927 he studied and earned a master's degree at the University of California, then went on to Oxford as a Rhodes Scholar and returned to the United States in 1930. He taught at a number of prestigious schools including Vanderbilt and Yale University. Robert Penn Warren remains the only writer ever to have received Pulitzer prizes for both fiction and poetry. His first Pulitzer was awarded for *All the King's Men* (1946), a novel of political corruption set in Louisiana. His poetry Pulitzers came from *Promises* (1957) and *Now and Then: Poems, 1978-1979.* Warren served as a Chancellor of the Academy of American Poets from 1972 until 1988, and was appointed the first U. S. Poet Laureate in 1985.

Thomas Wolfe (1900–1938) was born in Asheville, North Carolina. At fifteen, Wolfe entered the University of North Carolina, where he edited the college magazine and newspaper. Graduating in 1920, Wolfe went to Harvard University to study and become a playwright. He received his M.A. degree from Harvard in 1922, and for six years taught English at New York University where, during his free time completed his famous first novel, *Look Homeward, Angel* (1929), a lyrical account of his youth in Asheville. He gave up teaching when he was awarded a Guggenheim Fellowship in 1930 and went to Europe, where he traveled widely and continued to write. Wolfe's other works include *Of Time and the River* (1935); *From Death to Morning* (1935), and *The Story of a Novel* (1936). Some of Wolfe's best work was published posthumously (after his death) as *The Web and the Rock* (1939); *You Can't Go Home Again* (1940), and *The Hills Beyond* (1941).

Acknowledgments *(continued from p. ii)*

Herschel Gower, executor of the Estate of Mildred Haun
"Why Can't I Take Love Easy" from *Master's Thesis* by Mildred Haun (Vanderbilt University, 1937) Reprinted by permission of Herschel Gower, executor of the Estate of Mildred Haun.

Paul Green Foundation
In Abraham's Bosom in *Paul Green: Five Plays of the South*, copyright 1963 by Paul Green, copyright renewed 1991 by the Paul Green Foundation. Used by permission of the Paul Green Foundation.

Harcourt Brace & Company
Excerpt from "Jordan's End" from *The Shadowy Third and Other Stories* by Ellen Glasgow, copyright 1923 by Doubleday, Page & Co., Inc. and renewed 1951 by First and Merchants National Bank of Richmond Virginia. "The Patented Gate and the Mean Hamburger" from *The Circus in the Attic and Other Stories*, copyright 1947 and renewed 1975 by Robert Penn Warren. Reprinted by permission of Harcourt Brace & Company.

HarperCollins Publishers, Inc.
From *In Country, A Novel* by Bobbie Ann Mason. Copyright © 1985 by Bobbie Ann Mason. Reprinted by permission of HarperCollins Publishers, Inc.

Houghton Mifflin Company
"Adios, Miss Em" from *Wellspring* by Janice Holt Giles. Copyright © 1957, 1958, 1963, 1975 by Janice Holt Giles. Reprinted by permission of Houghton Mifflin Company. All rights reserved.

Alfred A. Knopf Inc.
"Parable of the Talents" from *The Future of the Race* by Henry Louis Gates Jr. and Cornel West. Copyright © 1996 by Henry Louis Gates Jr. and Cornel West. Reprinted by permission of Alfred A. Knopf Inc.

George Ella Lyon
Excerpt from "Voiceplace" by George Ella Lyon, from *Bloodroot: Reflections on Place by Appalachian Women Writers*, ed. Joyce Dyer. University Press of Kentucky, 1998. This essay first appeared in a slightly different form in Ohio Journal of the English Language Arts, 34, no. 2, Fall 1993. Reprinted by permission of the author.

Mary Ellen Miller, literary executor for the Estate of Jim Wayne Miller
"Squirrel Stand" from *Dialogue With A Dead Man* by Jim Wayne Miller. Copyright © 1974 by the University of Georgia Press. Used by permission of Mary Ellen Miller, Literary Executor.

William Morris Agency, Inc. on behalf of the Author
"Caribou" and "If Snakes Were Blue" from *New and Selected Poems, 1923-1985* by Robert Penn Warren. Copyright © 1985 by Robert Penn Warren. Reprinted by permission of William Morris Agency, Inc. on behalf of the Author.

W.W. Norton & Company, Inc.
"Hardweed Path Going," from *Collected Poems 1951-1971* by A.R. Ammons. Copyright © 1972 by A.R. Ammons. Reprinted by permission of W.W. Norton & Company, Inc.

Jesse Stuart Foundation
"Our Heritage," from *God's Oddling*, and excerpt from *Wild Plums*, from *A Jesse Stuart Reader* by Jesse Stuart. Copyright © 1963 McGraw Hill Book Company, Inc. Copyright © renewed 1991 Jesse Stuart Foundation. Used by permission of Jesse Stuart Foundation, P.O. Box 391, Ashland, KY 41114.

Russell & Volkening as agents for the author
"All That Glisters Isn't Gold" from *The Astronomer and Other Stories* by Doris Betts. Copyright © 1965 by Doris Betts, renewed 1994 by Doris Betts. Reprinted by the permission of Russell & Volkening as agents for the author.

Scribner, a division of Simon & Schuster
"The Far and the Near" and from "The Four Lost Men" reprinted with the permission of Scribner, a division of Simon & Schuster from *Death to Morning* by Thomas Wolfe. Copyright 1935 by Charles Scribner's Sons; copyright renewed © 1963 by Paul Gitlin, C.T.A. Administrator.

Joe Survant
"The Fish" by Joe Survant, originally appeared in *The Kentucky Review.* Copyright © Joe Survant. Reprinted by permission of the author.

University of Georgia Press
"An April Day" and "Memories" from *Joseph Seamon Cotter, Jr.: Complete Poems* by James Robert Payne. Copyright © 1990 by the University of Georgia Press. Reprinted by permission of University of Georgia Press.

University of Minnesota Press
"Lee in the Mountains" by Donald Davidson from *Poems 1922-1961* (University of Minnesota Press,) pp. 43-46. Copyright © 1924, 1927, 1934, 1935, 1938, 1952, 1961, 1966 by Donald Davidson. Reprinted by permission of University of Minnesota Press.

Viking Penguin, a division of Penguin Putnam Inc.
"On the Mountainside" by Elizabeth Madox Roberts, from *The Haunted Mirror* by Elizabeth Madox Roberts. Copyright 1932 by Elizabeth Madox Roberts; renewed 1960 by Ivor S. Roberts. Used by permission of Viking Penguin, a division of Penguin Putnam Inc.

Markus Wiener Publishing
From "Narrative of William Wells Brown" from *The Travels of William Wells Brown,* edited by Paul Jefferson. Reprinted by permission of Markus Wiener Publishing.

Note: Every effort has been made to locate the copyright owner of material reprinted in this book. Omissions brought to our attention will be corrected in subsequent editions.